THE ART OF MANIPULATION

Everything You Should Know About Psychology, Empathy and Persuasion Techniques to Convince and Manipulate Anyone Using Dark Psychology to Influence Human Behavior

Robert Covert

TABLE OF CONTENTS

INTRODUCTION

WHAT IS MANIPULATION?

To those who aren't fully aware of manipulation and what it is all about, it is hard to see that this process takes up three steps. Most of us will just think of manipulation as one thing—there needs to be two things in addition to the act of manipulation, which will make sure that the manipulation is successful. These include the analysis, which happens first; and the persuasion, which is going to take place for most of the conversation with the victim but is especially going to show up *after* the manipulation.

Understanding that there is more to the art of manipulation than just the act of manipulation itself is going to help you understand more about what can make the process more successful. While beginners may think that they can do it without the persuasion and the analysis aspects, you will quickly find that the results aren't as good if you miss these two parts and that you are less likely to get the things that you want.

When it comes to manipulation, it seems that a lot of people underestimate how powerful it can be—and oftentimes, they will misunderstand what is going on with this art form. It is common to see the word manipulation and believe automatically that the other person is trying to be emotionally abusive, mean, and cruel. We automatically associate a lot of negative traits back to the words.

While people can negatively use manipulation, it is important to remember that there are some positive parts of manipulation as well. Because so many people see manipulation as a negative thing, it can prevent them from realizing just how powerful of a psychological art form manipulation can be. Furthermore, many people fail to understand that pretty much each of us already uses manipulation in one manner or another—just by living our day-to-day lives. While we may not automatically see this kind of behavior as manipulation, we all will have some degree of practice with using it.

Learning how to manipulate effectively doesn't mean that you are heading out into the world and trying to create some abusive patterns between yourself and those around you. Instead, it just means that you know what you want, and you have refined the method that you want to use to get it. When it is all said and done, if someone doesn't want to give in to what you want, they won't.

Manipulation isn't all about the pressure put on the other person. The best manipulators don't force someone into doing something that they don't want to do. Instead, it is more about helping someone see the value in helping you and doing what you would like and then building up from there.

Before we start to look at some of the techniques that you can use with manipulation, we first need to dig deeper into what manipulation is all about, how and why manipulation tends to work, and when you would decide to work with manipulation in your own life.

CHAPTER 1: TYPES OF MANIPULATORS

While the common result expanded from each manipulation may look similar to the amount of control, there are various ways to get there. An individual trying to get something from you will do a multitude of maneuvers to get there, possibly even a combination of the different types we have here. As you may be able to tell while reading, not all manipulators are evil at heart, and some may even be acting on what they believe to be your best interest. Moving forward, it'll be beneficial to interpret which type of manipulator you're dealing with, and the best ways to overcome them.

"The Helpless" are individuals who can never seem to help themselves. It's perfectly okay to ask for help, but these individuals make a habit of it. The smallest amount of stress can send this person into a tailspin, and they become unable to help themselves. The task in question could be a variety of actions, but the main idea within this person's mind is that they are unwilling to deal with their own responsibilities. They'd much rather influence someone else to handle it for them. "The Helpless" often takes the form of a friend but could just as easily be someone closer such as a significant other or a relative. She has a child to take care of, and even though her childcare fell through, she's unwilling to stay home. Instead, she'd rather have another person take care of her responsibilities for her. It's quite alright to ask for help, but she continually asks as if she has no other option but for you to agree to babysit. In actuality, she could just as easily cancel her date and be the one to watch her child. This behavior leads to the ones around you eventually seeing through the helpless act, pushing you away. On the flip side, the ones who tend to fall for these acts are kind at heart, so it can be difficult to see through the mask. Take time to check in with yourself, ask yourself of the true intentions behind the ones who are constantly relying on you for things. You may find that to them, it's much easier to have you handle the important aspects of their life.

"Wordsmiths" are artists of the human language, always saying things in just the right way. This type of manipulator makes sure to say things so that they can't be held accountable for what they've said. They may tell you that they're going to meet you at the movie theater at nine, only to turn around and not show up, exclaiming they had said they MAY meet you at the movie theater at nine. If you become upset by this, the finger will often be pointed back in your direction. They'll make it seem as if it was your fault for the misunderstanding, and they had nothing to do with it. A wordsmith can always flip it the opposite direction, interjecting words into your speech to make it seem as if you've said something you hadn't.

Using the same example, maybe you had told your friend you'd see about meeting them at the movie theater. A wordsmith would show up to the theater, possibly even buy two tickets, and later explain how you had left them at the theater waiting for you. You never told them you were able to make it, but the "Wordsmith" will twist the words used to make it seem like you did. Unless you can recall word for word what was said, the "Wordsmith" often wins the battle, and you feel bad for bailing on your friend, regardless. This tactic can be used so that later it can be brought up again, to manipulate your behavior through guilt. You've always got to watch the way you say things around someone who plays with words in such a way, but you also can't always policy your words.

Many children couldn't fathom such a thing, but parental manipulation is also very common. Most of the time, both parents and children have no idea it's happening. This occurs because parents impose their own opinions, wants, and dreams onto their child. This can look like a parent pushing you to go to college to become a doctor, because they never went to college, or maybe pushing you to follow in the family business like your ancestors before you. Most want to make their parents proud, so it allows you to forget your dreams in the process of putting a smile on their faces. Parental manipulation also works the same when you're referencing in-laws. There's also this pressure that your significant other's family puts onto your family, that makes you feel like you must live up to their expectations. Common subjects are wedding details, when you're going to be having a baby, who is going to be the parent to stay home with that baby, etc. There's an overwhelming desire to not only not disappoint your parents, but also the parents of the person you love. Of course, our parents don't mean to manipulate us in this way, and usually, don't realize they have such a hold on us. It's natural for them to express their hopes and dreams for their children, but it crosses into different territory when it becomes overbearing or controlling. When confronted with these situations, it's important to remember your ideals and goals, or you can quickly become lost within someone else's.

Unrealistic promises are another common manipulation type that plays on your guilt. Your character is called into question, making you promise something you didn't want to do, or worse, couldn't promise to do. These situations happen spur of the moment, so you don't have time to think. Occasionally, you may have even told the other person about an event coming up, but they act as if they didn't know, manipulating you into committing your time to something else. We tend to go with the flow of the conversation, especially if we are distracted or having a good time. If you cancel, you'll be guilt-tripped and quite often put on the line for something else down the road. You don't want to enter the endless circle of guilt and obligation to someone. If this happens to you and you end up double-booked, try your best to keep your word this time. That way the situation doesn't continue anymore, and you can use it as a lesson moving forward to think before agreeing to something.

When someone asks something of you, it's alright to tell them you need some time, and you'll get back to them. A true friend will understand if you need to check your calendar first. This will also give you a bit of a hint as to whether they were trying to manipulate you or not. A way that a manipulator could work around this, is to get you to commit to a rushed promise. Did they become upset simply because you told them you needed time? Odds are, they were only out to get something from you to begin with.

Many of us have come across a "Blamer" in our life, and many of us have fallen into their trap. The blamer is not only known for not being able to take responsibility for their mistakes but often seeks to displace that blame somewhere else. Common phrases from Blamers are, "you made me do this" and "because of you". A blamer can take an argument you had with someone, later exclaiming that you made them late for work. Realistically, they could have ended the conversation or simplified it in some way. The argument continued of that person's own accord but is now attempting to shift blame. Blamers are also known to react rather quickly, which leads them to do and say things that they might regret later. These kinds of manipulators are often very impulsive and will say result to insults when they aren't getting their way. The arguments become heated very quickly, and it's best to take a step back and let yourself breath. Don't allow yourself to be wrapped up within the Blamer tactics and remember to take a breather. The extra time allotted to think access the situation will give you a clear mind of the events taking place. Are you finding that you're being blamed for situations that aren't your fault, or not? Is the individual trying to use your guilt against you? If so then you may have found yourself dealing with a Blamer. Not surprisingly, these are the most common manipulators because of the ease involved with pointing the finger elsewhere.

Another type of manipulator is referred to as the "Cost of Gratitude". As with most friends and relationships, you're bound to enter some sort of argument or disagreement at some point. This is normal between individuals and can easily be amended if the parties involved desire so. However, the manipulator almost makes these disagreements occur, and then plays the victim as if they're the most hurt by it. Not only do you need to apologize, but it's also going to take much more to earn their forgiveness. This is where the cost comes in because it truly is up to the manipulator as to how much your cost is going to be. These individuals seize the moment and play up the situation. Because it's only normal for people to desire an end to an altercation, the person being manipulated is willing to do anything they can to make amends. This can be in the form of money, a new gift, promising to attend a certain event, etc. As the person who was manipulated continues none the wiser.

Our next type is something like a wordsmith, but they focus on a few select words to get their point across. "It's better If" - are people who phrase things as if you've only got two choices in the entire world, and one is better than the other. For instance, if you've told your friend that you're unable to go to the movies tonight, they could answer that it's better if you go out with them than staying home. You never really explained what your other option was, or why you couldn't make it, but the manipulator will make up a boring second option and trick your mind. Of course, going out to a movie is better than staying at home. Even if you had planned on attending a date that night or had been thinking about participating in another activity such as bowling, your mind has been made to believe there were only two options. This is a false way to make someone believe that there are only two options when there are multiple.

The next few can be seen as a set, or even a group, depending on how you want to look at it. The "adult child" is someone who has yet to grow up yet. There can be people who still enjoy things that a child might enjoy, such as certain TV shows or video games, but this manipulation goes further. The adult child is consistently looking for their parents to support them and refuse to grow up. They may live at home, even if it's not out of necessity, and manipulate their parents into taking care of them. This feeds off the love of a parent and can go a step further. The adult child isn't only looking to be taken care of by their parents but can get anyone to fill the role of their parent. Usually, this takes place within relationships more than anything. The manipulator can be a male or female if they are being taken care of. An example of this would be a male and a female meet online playing a popular video game. They begin an online relationship, where the male ends up moving out of his parents' house and begins living with the female. He refuses to get a job, continually playing the same video game even when his girlfriend is at work all day, now supporting the pair of them. If she were to lose her job for some reason, he'd leave in a heartbeat, because he's realized he was no longer going to be taken care of. The stereotype with these manipulators is that they tend to be females taking advantage of males but can just as easily happen the other way around.

The last manipulator type we will cover can be referred to as a "Triangulator". These are the type of people that will always involve a third person and get them on their side. They're quick to say something nasty and will often call out someone else to back them up. These thoughts may have been expressed to them in some capacity, but usually not in the way the third person intended. This drives a wedge between two people that could otherwise be good friends, or even family members, because of the manipulation technique being used. If you've ever been in an argument with a potential manipulator, and they call out a third person, then you'll already have experience with this manipulator type. A good person, or a good friend, wouldn't bring a third person into the mix, and definitely wouldn't mention them by name. This only serves to create more conflict where it's not needed and cause more hurt upon the person they're trying to manipulate. Your anger is dispersed between the manipulator, as well as the third person. A good triangulator will also work on the other side of the situation, meaning they could also be telling secrets or spreading lies about you to the third person. Usually, this is how they get people to speak badly about one another, by twisting the truth and spreading lies.

No matter the type of manipulator you come across, know that they only seek to influence and control you. There are multiple different ways that they can accomplish this, and what led them down this path, but the goal of every manipulator is the same. These specific types will give you an idea of who you are dealing with, and the reasons behind it, but it's not going to stop their manipulating ways. Use this as an outline for help but know that you will need help if you plan on keeping this person in your life at all. This may come in the form of therapy for this person, and even yourself if you find that you're the manipulator in the relationship.

CHAPTER 2: HOW AND WHY DOES MANIPULATION WORK?

Despite what it may seem, manipulation is going to work easily. For the most part, people are going to be automatically wired to say no to something the first time that they hear about it, especially if whoever is asking the question is someone the victim doesn't know or trust already—when it is someone that the victim trusts, they are more likely to really think about the question and there is a higher odd of them saying yes.

Let's assume for a moment that you don't already know the other person and that you haven't been able to build up their trust before you work to manipulate them. As a result, any time that you ask the other person for something, they are just going to tell you no.

The idea that comes with this one is pretty simple. We do not typically like to take things from people who we do not have trust in. It is sort of like taking candy from a stranger or letting a stranger do something for you that could potentially leave you vulnerable and exposed to some sort of threat. These are things that we just wouldn't do. When someone we don't really know or trust asks you for something, there is always going to be that natural inclination to say no to them because we don't have enough trust and history with this person to know what the result isn't going to be devastating in one way or another for us in the end.

The same is going to be true of others when you try to manipulate them. If you ask someone for a favor, there is a high chance that they will also say no to you, unless you already know them and have built up trust with them. Of course, there are steps that you can take that can help you build up those feelings a bit quicker so that you can get that yes much faster. With some practice and a bit more knowledge about the different manipulation techniques, you will be able to manipulate others and get a yes from them in no time.

BAD MANIPULATION

There are a lot of different types of manipulation that are available throughout the world—and often, we are going to think about the bad form of manipulation. This is because most of us have heard about manipulation from books, movies, and the news. These sources are just going to spend time talking about manipulation and all of the bad things that had happened when someone used manipulation.

How many times, for example, have you turned on the television and heard about some group or cult who took advantage of someone, or maybe a smaller group of people, and gotten them to change their whole personalities and more? You may have heard about some people being willing to kill, attack, and do more, even though they were the calmest and most controlled person in the world before this all happens.

Now, this is a little extreme, but there are many times when the manipulation is going to be seen as a negative thing. When this happens, it usually is because the manipulator is looking to get what they want, to gain something, without caring what happens to the other person. They may even want the target to become dependent on them to ensure that they can come back and use that person as often as they would like.

The target in this situation is often going to be the one who is harmed or hurt in some manner. Whether they are physically harmed in the process, or they are just led to believe that they aren't worth anything at all, you will find that it can be damaging to the target. The one person who is going to be able to benefit from this kind of manipulation is the manipulator.

WHEN WOULD I NEED TO MANIPULATE SOMEONE?

There are actually quite a few times when you would have the desire to manipulate someone else. One example of this is a salesperson who wants to make a sale. Through the use of some of the strategies we will talk about for manipulation, the salesperson would be able to develop any opportunities that are needed to easily and quickly established a rapport. Once that rapport is set up, they will find that the sale with the victim, or the customer, in this case, is going to lose quickly.

People are much less likely to give you the answer of no when they trust you, and you can get them to take the time to listen to your offer. This can also be true when it comes to making any recommendations as needed, requesting someone to come help you, and pretty much any other time that you are trying to get your way. The idea is that if you would like to convince someone else to get what you want, you will make sure that you are never harmful to someone else in the process, you could use manipulation to help you get the thing that you want.

WHEN SHOULD I AVOID MANIPULATING SOMEONE?

Despite all the power that can come with manipulation, there are going to be some times when you shouldn't use it at all. You will find that people, can't be manipulated unless there is some willingness for this to happen. If you come across someone who is completely against agreeing with you and doing what you are asking them to do, there is no way that you can come in and change their mind without calling on manipulation tactics that are often seen as abusive, cruel, and harsh.

If you want to master the art of manipulation, you must make sure that the delicate boundaries are kept, and that you work on the right strategies, without being harmful to the other person in the process. There are going to be times when the victim says no to you, and as the manipulator, you need to respect the no that they give.

Of course, this doesn't mean that you have to give up completely, you could still call on some of the tactics of persuasion to see if you can organically get the other person to change their mind. However, you should not try to force the other person to change their mind or opinion. When you try to force your ideas on the other person, this is where the idea of manipulation starts to turn into a bad thing that needs to be avoided.

CHAPTER 3: WHAT IS COVERT EMOTIONAL MANIPULATION?

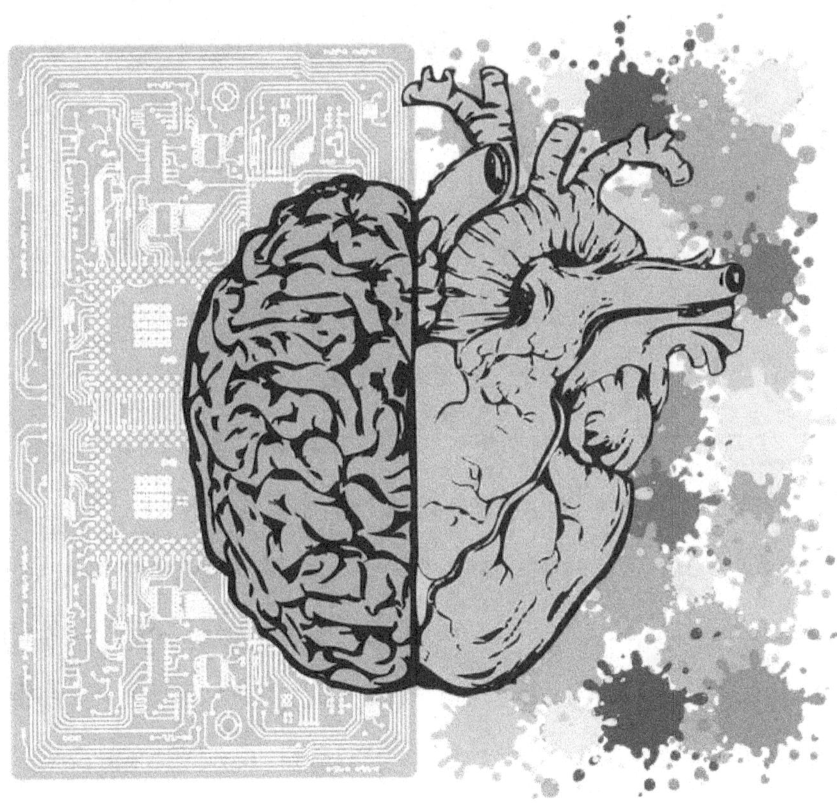

Covert emotional manipulation is used by people who want to gain power or control over you by deploying tactics that are both deceptive and underhanded. Such people want to change the way you think and behave without you ever realizing what it is they are doing. In other words, they use techniques that can alter your perceptions in such a way that you think that you are doing it out of your own free will. Covert emotional manipulation is "covert" because it works without you being consciously aware of that fact. People who are good at deploying such techniques can get you to do their bidding without your knowledge; they can hold you "psychologically captive."

When skilled manipulators set their sights on you, they can get you to grant them power over your emotional well-being and even your self-worth. They will put you under their spell without you even realizing it. They will win your trust, and you will start attaching value to what they think of you. Once you have let them into your life, they will then start chipping away at your very identity in a methodical way, and as time goes by you will lose your self-esteem and turn into whatever they want you to be.

Covert emotional manipulation is more common than you might think. Since it's subtle, people are rarely aware that it's happening to them, and in some cases, they may never even notice. Only keen outside observers may be able to tell when this form of manipulation is going on.

You might know someone who used to be fun and jovial, then she got into a relationship with someone else, and a few years down the line, she seems to have a completely different personality. If it's an old friend, you might not even recognize the person she has become. That is how powerful covert emotional manipulation can be. It can completely overhaul someone's personality without them even realizing it. The manipulator will chip away at you little by little, and you will accept minute changes that fly under the radar, until the old you are replaced by a different version of you, build to be subservient to the manipulator.

Covert emotional manipulation works like a slow-moving coup. It requires you to make small progressive concessions to the person that is trying to manipulate you. In other words, you let go of tiny aspects of your identity to accommodate the manipulative person, so it never registers in your mind that there is something bigger at play.

When the manipulative person pushes you to change in small ways, you will comply because you don't want to "sweat the small stuff." However, there is a domino effect that occurs as you start conceding to the manipulative person. You will be more comfortable making subsequent concessions, and your personality will be erased and replaced in a cumulative progression.

Covert emotional manipulation occurs to some extent in all social dynamics. Let's look at how it plays out in romantic relationships, in friendships, and at work.

EMOTIONAL MANIPULATION IN RELATIONSHIPS

There is a lot of emotional manipulation that takes place in romantic relationships, and it's not always malicious. For example, women try to modify men's behavior to make them more "housebroken"; that is just normal. However, there are certain instances of manipulation where the person's intention is malicious, and he/she is motivated by a need to control or dominate over the other person.

Positive reinforcement is perhaps the most used covert manipulation technique in romantic relationships. Your partner can get you to do what he wants by praising you, flattering you, giving you attention, offering your gifts, and acting affectionately.

Even the seemingly nice things in relationships can turn out to be covert manipulation tools and props. For instance, your girlfriend could use intense sex as a weapon to reinforce a certain kind of behavior in you. Similarly, men can use charm, appreciation, or gifts to reinforce certain behaviors in the women they are dating.

Some sophisticated manipulators use what psychologists call "intermittent positive reinforcement" to gain control over their partners. The way it works is that the perpetrator will shower the victim with intense positive reinforcement for a certain period of time, then switch to just giving her normal levels of attention and appreciation. After a random interval of time, he will again go back to the intense positive reinforcement. When the victim gets used to the special treatment, it's taken away, and when she gets used to normal treatment, the special treatment is brought back, and it all seems arbitrary. Now, the victim will get to a place where she becomes sort of "addicted" to the special treatment, but she has no idea how to get it, so she starts doing whatever the perpetrator wants in the hope that one of the things she does will bring back the intense positive reinforcement. In other words, she effectively becomes subservient to the perpetrator.

Negative reinforcement techniques are also used in relationships to manipulate others covertly. For example, partners can withhold sex as a way of compelling the other person to modify their behavior in a specific way. People also use techniques such as the silent treatment, and withholding of love and affection.

Some malicious people can create a false sense of intimacy by pretending to open up to you. They could share personal stories and talk about their hopes and fears. When they do this, they create the impression that they trust you, but their intention may be to get you to feel a sense of obligation towards them.

Manipulators also use well-calculated insinuations to get you to react in a certain way at the moment, to modify your behavior in the long run. Such insinuations can be made through words or even actions. In colloquial terms, we call this "dropping a hint." People in relationships are always trying to figure out what the other person wants out of that relationship, so a manipulative person can drop hints to get you to do what they want without ever having to take responsibility for the actions that you take because they can always argue that you misinterpreted what they meant.

However, malicious insinuations can be very hurtful, and they can chip away at your self-esteem. Your partner can insinuations to suggest you are gaining weight, you aren't making enough money, or even to suggest that your cooking skills aren't any good. People use insinuations to get away with "saying without saying," any number of hurtful things that could affect your self-esteem.

EMOTIONAL MANIPULATIONS IN FRIENDSHIPS

Covert emotional manipulation is quite common in friendships and casual relationships. Friendships tend to progress slower than romantic relationships, but that just means that it can take a lot more time for you to figure out if your friends are manipulative. Manipulation in friendships can be confusing because even well-meaning friends can come across as malicious. That's because there is a certain social rivalry that exists between even the closest of friends, which explains the concept of "frenemies."

Manipulative friends tend to be passive-aggressive. This is where they manipulate you into doing what they want by involving mutual friends rather than by coming to you directly. Passive aggression works as a manipulation technique because it denies you a chance of directly addressing whatever issue your friend is raising, and so in a manner of speaking, you lose by default.

For example, if a friend wants you to do her a favor, instead of coming out and asking you, she goes to a mutual friend and suggests that she asks you on her behalf. Now, when the mutual friend approaches you, it becomes very difficult for you to turn down the request because there is added social pressure. When you say no, your whole social circle now perceives you as selfish.

Passive aggression can also involve the use of silent treatment to get you to comply with a request. Imagine a situation where one of your friends talks to everyone else but you. It's going to be incredibly awkward for you, and everyone will start prying, wondering what the issue is between the two of you, and taking sides on the matter.

Friends can also covertly manipulate you by using subtle insults. They can give you back-handed compliments that have hidden meanings. When you take the time to think about what they meant by the compliment, you will realize that it's an insult in disguise, and that will bruise your self-esteem, and possibly modify your behavior.

Some friends can manipulate you by going on a "power trip" and trying to control your social interactions. For example, there are those friends who are going to insist that every time you hang out, it should be in their apartment, or at a social venue of their choosing. Such friends often have the intention of dominating your friendship, so they are keen to always have the "home ground advantage" over you. They'll try to push you out of your comfort zone, just so that you can reveal your weaknesses and you can then become more emotionally reliant on them.

Manipulative friends tend to excessively capitalize on your friendship, and to a disproportionate degree. They will ask you for lots of favors with no regard for your time or your effort. They are the kinds of friends who will leverage your friendship every time they need something, but then make excuses when it's their turn to reciprocate.

EMOTIONAL MANIPULATION AT WORK

There are many reasons why your colleague may want to manipulate you. It could be you are on the same career path, and so he wants to make you look bad. It could be that he is lazy and he wants to stick you with his responsibilities. It could also be that he is a sadist and he just wants to see you suffer.

One-way people at work exert their dominance over others is by stressing them out and then, almost immediately, relieving the stress. Say, for example, you make a minor error on a report, and your boss calls you into his office. He makes a big fuss and threatens to fire you, but then towards the end, he switches gears and reassures you that your job is secure as long as you do what he wants. That kind of manipulation works on people because it makes them afraid and gives them a sense of obligation at the same time.

Some colleagues can manipulate you by doing you small favors, and then reminding you of those favors every time they want something from you. For instance, if you made an error at work and a colleague covered for you, he may hold it over your head for months or even years to come, and he is going to guilt you into feeling indebted to him.

Colleagues can also manipulate you by leaving you out of the loop when they are passing across important information. The intention here is to get you to mess up so that they can have a better standing with the boss or with other colleagues. When you discover that someone is leaving you out of the loop at work and you confront them, they could feign innocence and pretend that it was a genuine mistake on their part, or they could find a way to turn it around and blame you.

People with dark personality traits tend to be hyper-competitive at work, and they won't hesitate to use underhanded means to pull one over you. Most colleagues turn out to be good friends, but you should be careful with colleagues that are overly eager to befriend you. It could be that they want to learn more about you so that they can figure out your strengths and weaknesses, and find ways to use them against you. Narcissists, Machiavellians, and psychopaths are very good at scheming at work, so don't let them catch you off guard.

CHAPTER 4: PERSUASION HISTORY

THE HISTORY OF PERSUASION AND HOW PEOPLE APPLIED TECHNIQUES IN ANCIENT TIMES

Persuasion has a long history, going back to when humans discovered how to use it to our advantage. Persuasion is defined as a type of behavior that is employed as a means to influence someone's way of thinking, beliefs, decisions, motivation, and behavior.

It can be subtle and undetectable, done covertly, or more obvious, such as a form of encouragement.

The reasons for persuasion vary and are commonly used for personal and/or financial gain. It's a method applied throughout history for political and social gain. One notable example is how the Greeks viewed forms of persuasion, as a way to measure the suitability of a politician or position of authority. The ability to persuade was valued highly, and those who were successful were regarded as worthy of election.

Aristotle, a Greek philosopher, regarded persuasion as an essential skill to acquire and develop for a variety of reasons. It can be argued that persuasion, if used in its most skillful form, can deflect a lot of negative attributes and help someone gain favor, regardless of the circumstance. An example of this is a court case, where a defendant or their lawyer can argue their innocence by way of persuasion. Even where a defendant is believed to be guilty, persuasion can (and has) convince a judge or jury that evidence is circumstantial or that a witness's testimony is not credible. There is more to this method than simply convincing an individual or group of a certain belief or concept with a smooth presentation and convincing words; it includes a far more in-depth study and observation of the people who are to be persuaded. Many of these attributes are useful in winning an argument or a case, whether the person employing the persuasion techniques is correct or not. In some cases, it's not about right or wrong, but instead, a variance in opinions or beliefs where persuasion can go a long way to convince people to see the other side of the debate.

WHAT ARE THE DIFFERENT TYPES OF PERSUASION?

Rhetoric is a powerful method of persuasion, which involves the careful study and observation of people, either in groups, as individuals or in society, to better understand how best to apply the "art" of persuasion. Observing people would entail a lot of studies, including employing skilled writers, artists, and speakers with the expertise and talent to persuade. A modern example of this method can be seen in advertisements aimed at specific demographics to promote the sale of a product, or a political campaign targeting undecided voters, to sway their decision one way or another.

The goal is not only to get your attention but to maintain it by "speaking" to you in a way that evokes an emotional response or action. This could result in an emotional plea to support one political party instead of others or to purchase a certain product or service because of a certain nostalgia or connection with family or co-workers.

The reasons for using persuasive techniques is not always secretive or malicious: it can be a good way to convince someone to reconsider making the wrong decision that could result in a detrimental outcome, or serve as a form of positive encouragement or reinforcement as a form of empowerment, such as "you can do it" and "what have you got to lose, come on!" When persuasion takes on a more direct tone, it may seem like a strong form of encouragement. While this may work for some people, it doesn't have the same impact on others. Some people thrive on overt persuasion and may otherwise not achieve a milestone or "go for it" without that persuasive push. On the other hand, some people prefer more autonomy and do not respond well. This is where covert or more subtle forms of persuasion can be useful in influencing them.

Recognizing the different signs of persuasion is key to knowing if someone is using these methods on you. It may not be as obvious as coaxing someone to change their mind or try something new. Some forms of persuasion may be subtle and difficult to detect initially.

Understanding the reasons behind persuasive techniques and the different purposes they serve can help determine if you may be on the receiving end and the reasons why.

THREE BASIC FORMS OF PERSUASION

There are three types of persuasion: ethos, logos, and pathos, according to Aristotle. Each method appeals to a different source and has its reason for use:

ETHOS

Ethos is known as the persuasion using ethics or morality as a basis. In this method of persuasion, the speaker or individual applying this method is trustworthy, credible, and knowledgeable. In their speech or debate, a credible person will make use of their related expertise and knowledge to support their argument. This is done by citing relevant sources and using their credibility as an expert to persuade the listener of their legitimacy.

This method is regarded as respectful in that it doesn't intend to sway the listener for unethical gain or advantage.

The speaker's reputation and status carry a lot of weight in terms of credibility, though this can also be established by using carefully constructed arguments that show that they are ethical.

LOGOS

Logos is based primarily in logic, or the application of logic to reason with or persuade someone. This method involves using evidence and related studies to support an argument.

It's a clear, concise form that doesn't convince someone based on pseudo-science or skewed facts, but rather, it appeals to people who are not easily persuaded unless facts and their related sources support the argument. The format of logos is usually presented in a clear, sometimes chronological and progressive manner to show how a subject or topic began as disputable, followed by studies and observation to gain factual information to support the argument.

PATHOS

Pathos is a method of persuasion that uses the emotion of the recipient (the person being persuaded). This is one of the most powerful and frequently used methods of persuasion. Pathos appeals to an audience's emotions, including their passions, imagination, creativity, and sympathetic nature. While the aim of this method is similar to logos and ethos, pathos can become very deceptive is using a vulnerable person's or group's emotions to their advantage. This can be seen in high control groups, where the promise of making lots of money or reaping the rewards of following a set of rules or belief system. Emotional persuasion can also be powerful in helping the audience identify with the speaker and/or their supporters, by sharing personal experiences and anecdotes that can convince people they are sincere and genuine, or "just one of us." The danger with employing pathos is how it can be misused to take advantage of a vulnerable or gullible group of people who are looking for quick answers and solutions to their problems.

ELEMENTS OF PERSUASION

There are characteristics of persuasion that can determine how successful the effect is on other people. These attributes are key in focusing attention on the listener or recipient of the persuasion, often to observe their reaction and level of engagement.

Some people are more easily convinced than others. Some people require a high degree of credibility and factual information before they will consider agreeing with a specific side of an argument. Others, on the other hand, are more easily swayed with far less effort.

LIKEABILITY

To persuade someone, they must like you or at least share a common ground. A company representative, for example, may not be successful in persuading or "selling" their products or reputation unless they first develop a rapport with their audience. Initially, a person in a representative position may seem intimidating or unrelatable, so they will often find common ground or likable traits to connect with people before they apply their persuasion techniques. An example, they may share an anecdotal story about their immediate family or personal experience that resonates with others.

This is essentially their "gateway" to establishing a connection and further their pitch.

Most people want to be liked. If an individual or group of people feel marginalized or ostracized in any way, a display of acceptance or being liked can feel empowering. Unfortunately, it can also pave a dangerous path to being taken advantage of, as the person showing approval may have malicious intentions of trying to swindle them or use their plight to their own advantage.

BUILDING TRUST

Without trust, there is no success in persuasion. People tend to question who they don't trust or agree with. If you are tasked with persuading someone to comply with the opposite side of their views, it will likely never happen, unless they have a great deal of trust and confidence in you. Even in cases where trust is established, persuasion can be challenging, though combined with other elements, it becomes easier. Building trust takes time and doesn't always happen immediately. If there are similarities between you and the person looking to gain your trust, it becomes an easier process. Once trust is established, the recipient of the persuasion may let their guard down and become more susceptible to influence than before. When you feel that someone is worthy of your trust, it's important to continually question and evaluate how they communicate, as it is common to become more comfortable and less cautious once that barrier of mistrust is lowered.

COMMUNICATION SKILLS

Using effective communication skills is important and tailoring the types of phrases and words used is vital to maintaining interest in persuasion. People will respond if you speak to them in familiar and understandable terms, instead of using elaborate descriptions and over-the-top speeches.

If people feel that they can understand and relate, and reciprocate on the same level, then persuasion becomes useful and powerful. People tend to be drawn to others who share similar experiences, beliefs, and ideas.

If someone is a smooth talker or conversationalist, they may also be a master of persuasion and should be approached with caution.

MAINTAINING CONSISTENCY

Keeping the conversation and expectations consistent from the beginning is important in maintaining engagement. When someone deviates from the initial goal, even with good persuasion skills, they lose followers and trust. A skilled speaker will keep things consistent, though it can be difficult to determine whether they are sincere in their goals (even with the ability to stay on track) or if their techniques are sharpened well enough to convince people of their legitimacy.

There are many other techniques and common strategies applied in persuasion, which will be covered in this book. Persuasion, in its basic form, can be effective as a tool for many people to achieve a goal or status in life. On the receiving end, it may have its benefits, where the intentions are good and ethical. Unfortunately, persuasion can often be used as a way to influence our emotions and behavior to the degree of mind control, which can lead to exploitation.

CHAPTER 5: EMOTIONAL INTELLIGENCE AND MANIPULATION

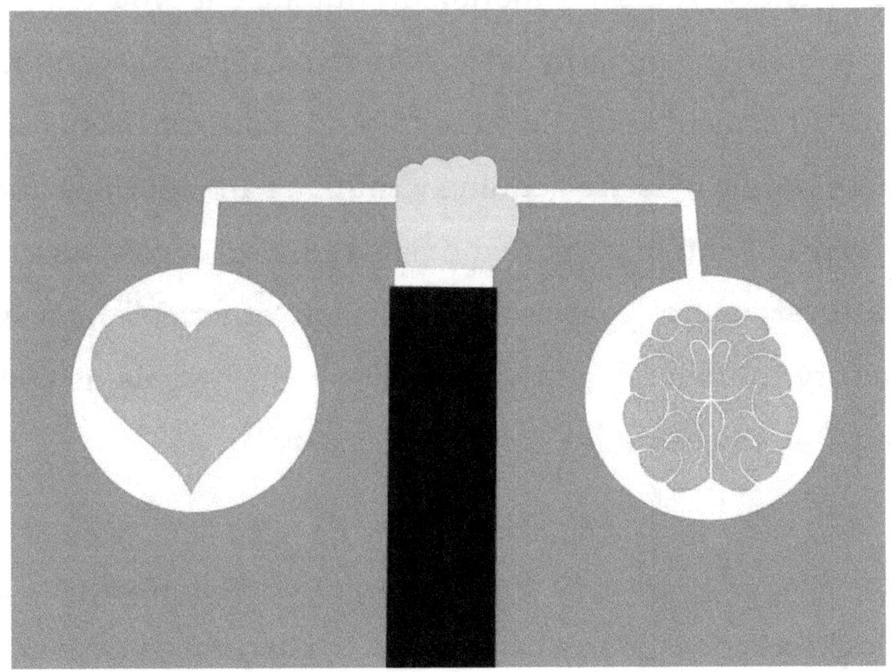

Emotional intelligence is about self-awareness, self-management, and relationship management. It's about understanding yourself and having the ability to manage your emotions, plus your response to those emotions.

However, although emotional intelligence can be learned, it isn't something you learn in a weekend program and be "covered" for the others of your life. That is a lifelong learning skill, that needs to be practiced and improved on throughout life.

To consider yourself emotionally intelligent, you should try to build up empathy which can make it easy to connect with others and know how they feel. Empathetic people are those people who are genuinely thinking about others and who readily offer support and help to those who require it. Not everyone can place themselves in other folks' shoes and try to understand their motives, which explains why empathy can be such a very important skill.

For this very reason, developing emotional intelligence should come easily to a person who is a natural empath or a people person. Others can find out about it in a course or from a created book, but as with most other abilities, to be proficient at it, you need to practice and apply emotional intelligence to as many situations as possible.

However, having high empathy is not easy. You need to be willing to listen in to various other person's feelings and attitudes, to try and understand their behavior, to pay attention without judgment, etc. Not everyone can do this, which explains why many believe that empathy is not a skill, but a natural gift.

In other words, emotionally intelligent people are not empathic only once it suits them, but all the time. This is probably why there are very few extremely empathic people around, although it's no secret that empathy could be faked, either to influence somebody or for self-promotion.

EMOTIONAL INTELLIGENCE

Emotional intelligence (also referred to as emotional quotient or EQ) refers to your developed capacity to identify, appreciate, control, and use emotions to advantage yourself as well as others confidently. This definition could be split into four basic categories:

- *Recognition: To become alert to your own emotions also to recognize your relationship with them.*

- *Appreciation: This can be the most difficult aspect to master since you must figure out how to appreciate your emotions for what they are. Only one time you accept them and find a genuine appreciation for them is it possible to move on to control them healthily.*

- *Control: Many people confuse this factor with the suppression of emotion. To suppress them is indeed a kind of control nonetheless it is forced and only short-term. Suppression leaves you more hurt and susceptible to eruption over time. The purpose here is to allow emotions to release in a controlled way so that they look for a healthy release beneficial to you as well as your interactions.*

- *Confidence: The final aspect of EQ where you can effectively use your emotions in conversation to relieve tension, pull through challenging conditions, resolve squabbles & dissensions, and be empathetic to others.*

Consequently, a strongly developed sense of emotional intelligence can help you establish and comprehend momentous and emotional episodes in the lives of those around you. At the smallest amount, emotional cleverness equips you having the ability to know your emotions, this is of these feelings, and the potential results your emotions have on those around you. The theory concept here is based on understanding and managing your emotions.

It is important to realize that emotional intelligence is a learned skill and not necessarily a birthright. To gain this skill, you have to train yourself. The good news is that you can sufficiently learn it anytime in your life, which is also why there is no need for a good reason to lack this essential skill!

Although most people generally know what emotions are, it is important to first define and understand exactly what is being referred to throughout this written publication.

WHAT ARE EMOTIONS?

There are varied definitions of emotions plus some existing literature attempts to compare emotions with feelings in a bid to justify which of both precedes the other. Taking all information and viewpoints into consideration, we can define emotions on three different levels.

- Physically: Feelings are reactions from the brain's subcortical sections in response to stimuli. These reactions generate biochemical responses within your body thus changing one's physical condition. They can, in turn, compel one to act on any matter that stirs the emotions in a threatening or enjoyable way. For this reason, they are seen as part of human survival instincts also.

- Mentally: Emotions are normal responses that provide rise to certain thoughts and circumstances of the mind, changing one's state of mind with regards to the stimuli. For this reason, our thoughts are influenced by emotions before we can even think of them often! It also dates back to remembering how someone or matter made you feel as the emotional memory space is stored for you to mentally think about down the road.

- Emotionally: This seems like an obvious one however the emotional component of emotions is usually oddly the hardest part for most people to grasp! It exists within us beyond the physical and mental elements somewhere. This is the primary emotion itself; what we feel, how we experience, and the role these feelings play inside our lives. Simply, it is the overall emotional condition of being.

Feelings create an endless response cycle between your physical body and brain for better or worse. They can control your activities or help enhance them - this all depends on your relationship with them and your emotional state to be. Overall, feelings are responses to different circumstances that go far beyond the physical features of chemicals releasing within the body.

Emotional senses range between cheerfulness, shock, and anxiety, to sorrow, hatred, and rage. Although feelings are an important part of human living, they may affect your conduct and sometimes, you can risk attaching feelings to everything.

Although these skills are essential for the workplace, they will help you improve your relationships outside of work also. To build up, and perfect, your emotional intelligence you need to start paying even more attention to emotions, yours' and others', start to pay attention more and talk less, and make an effort to become more available to other people's viewpoints.

4 TIPS ABOUT HOW TO DEVELOP EMOTIONAL INTELLIGENCE

Get to know yourself

Try to realize why you feel a certain way, and what had triggered such feelings. When the triggers are known by you, you can either prevent certain situations or, if they're unavoidable, find a real way of dealing with them. Understanding triggers help deepen your self-consciousness because this can help you learn how certain situations, emotions or people cause you to feel, and why. You must learn to never ignore your emotions, even negative ones, but to identify them and cope with them.

Try to understand others

Unfortunately, most of us are often too busy for treatment. Life has become extremely complicated and competitive, because of which, just maintaining your head above water is normally a challenge, aside from sharing what small spare energy or time you have with others.

Besides, in the Western culture, along with in societies where there is a high turnover of people and staff constantly maneuver around, changing jobs and cities they live in regularly, most of the associations are superficial and based on interest. To understand someone else's motives and feelings, you need to be willing to devote your undivided mind and attention to that person. You have to want to understand their behavior and attitude, to listen attentively all night if you have to, to be content for them, or become sad with them.

This is often particularly hard in case you are working with someone who is filled with long-held anger or frustration. So, although empathy can be developed with perseverance and great listening skills, those people who are naturally caring and compassionate will be the most empathetic.

Think that before you speak

Once you identify your emotion and know what had triggered it, take some time to comprehend it and "procedure" it, before responding to it. Basically, allow it to sink in before you react. If overwhelmed with emotions, it may help to ask yourself why you feel the true way you do. When you know why something had produced you feel angry, betrayed or embarrassed, it becomes much easier deciding what the next step should be.

Learn about the importance of self-management

If you figure out how to identify, control, and express your emotions, you should understand how to use them in ways that's most effective under the situations. Many people underestimate the importance of expressing their feelings in an adult way. Like ignoring or repressing emotions is bad for your health just, so is overreacting, ie expressing emotions without the consideration for how they may affect others.

Therefore, continue reminding yourself that although held-back emotions create tension, both and externally internally, those expressed in a rush and without thinking are like shooting without aiming. The ultimate way to improve your self-management is to have significantly more psychological self-control and constantly work on enhancing your integrity.

CHAPTER 6: HOW THE HUMAN BRAIN WORKS

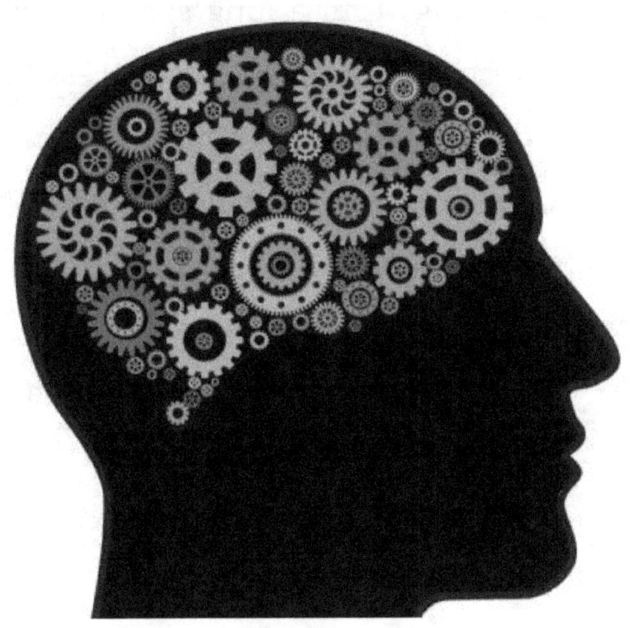

Psychology seeks to clarify the human behavior and cognitive process by the interaction of human behavior and cognitive process at a systematic level. Thus, the sphere of scientific discipline is tightly tangled with the study of the brain. Currently, we tend to come back to debate initially that however the evolution and heredity affects the human behavior

EVOLUTION AND HEREDITY

According to biological specialists the organism existing these days area unit outcome of the method of evolution that has been happening from a long span of your time. The body and pattern of behavior that's accessible these days is a result or consequence of evolution and as per this read of evolution, the foremost acceptable issue that comes out this development is an adaptation to the atmosphere that is central to the method of evolution. The traits and behavior that change an organism to survive area unit maintained et al. area unit destroyed that called the method of natural action.

There are unit options that distinguish a personality's being with different species those area unit bodily property, that's ability to steer upright, the second is encephalization that increases in brain size and proportion of specialized brain tissue and therefore, the third one is the development of language that may be a key to effective communication and cultural accomplishment of person. Except for these variations, there's the atmosphere that makes parity among the person. The atmosphere suggests that after we talk about the person in society and therefore, society is even the whole world for a living person. However, once it involves scientific discipline, the atmosphere is restricted for each individual as an example, the atmosphere inside the mother's uterus and it plays a really necessary role in determinative the behavior and temperament development of a private.

The home atmosphere, parental love, and feeling, association with relation, neighbors, peers, teachers, etc. can produce a wholly completely different and new atmosphere. This is often referred to as the social atmosphere. All the social factors expressed on top of the form the temperament of the kid.

Heredity, we'd like to understand initial that what's heredity? It refers to the genetic inheritance or endowment that a personality's body gets from their oldsters usually that is termed biological blueprint. Within the terms of science, a person's order interacts with the atmosphere to influence the behavior. The physical characteristics like height, weight, color of eye and skin, social and intellectual behavior area unit determined by the issue of heredity. Variations within these characteristics area unit thanks to the amendment in the genes transmitted that area of unit basic variations in human look. As an example, fraternal twins additionally disagree with one another, as a result of which they're born out of various genes.

THE CELL

It is the littlest unit of frame or we are able to say this is often the bottom for creation of person as an example the brick is that the smallest unit in an exceedingly building construction in same means cell is that the smallest unit of living being whether or not it's plant, person or animals, all area unit created up with cells.

THE NEURON

The cells that compose system and nervous area unit referred to as neurons, these neurons transmit info from one location to a different one. These nerve cells collect info from the atmosphere by suggests that of receptors then mix the knowledge furthermore as build the action attainable. Additional we are going to discuss regarding brain

THE BRAIN

If you would like to own body of the brain you would possibly study this section additionally, the innermost structure of the brain is that the half that is nearest to neural structure and area unit the oldest a part of the brain these areas perform identical perform they did it for our ancestors. Typically, this a part of the brain regulates basic perform of survival like respiration, moving, resting, feeding and our emotions too. Humans have a massive and developed outer layer that's referred to as "cerebral cortex" it makes the USA notably adept at these processes.

The brain is primarily a part of the central system and nervous, occupying the bodily cavity and is encircled by bone for defense. The burden of the brain is 3 pounds as a mean that comprises ninety-seven % of the entire central system and nervous. By connected through the higher finish of neural structure it's 3 structures that area unit having their functions, those area unit neural structure, neural structure and brain stem that is resulting in neural structure. The brain stem is additionally additional divided into the neural structure, the neural structure, and therefore, the Pons Varolii.

CEREBRAL CORTEX

The upmost layer of the brain known as neural structure, it creates consciousness and thinking. The key to the advance intelligence of soul than alternative living beings isn't truly the larger size of the human brain however it what set humans except alternative living beings is our larger neural structure. In soul, this half is wrinkled and collapsible and divided into 2 hemispheres and separated by folds referred to as fissures. Every hemisphere is split into four lobes.

We see initial the lobe (behind the forehead), that is accountable primarily for thinking, planning, memory, and judgment in the soul. Following the lobe is that the lobe and that extends from the center to the rear of the bone and that is accountable primarily for process info concerning bit. Then we tend to come to the lobe at the back of the bone and that processes visual info. Finally, before the lobe (pretty a lot of between the ears) is that the lobe and that is accountable primarily for hearing and language.

The human brain is structured on a general principle, known as contralateral management suggests that every hemisphere process, info concerning the other aspect of the body. For instance, after you write together with your right-hand, the motor info sanctionative your manus to maneuver comes from your hemisphere. We will say the brain is wired such in most cases the hemisphere receives sensations from it and it controls the correct aspect of the body, and contrariwise.

THE LOBES OF NEURAL STRUCTURE

There are centers in these lobes that are liable for awareness of surroundings and responses to the amendment in surroundings even.

Any visual info is taken primarily by the visual area that is found in the lobe. Same because it senses modality info is received by primary cortical area settled in lobe, more the data from body senses are received by the sensory system cortex that's settled within the lobe. The correct and left cerebral hemispheres of cortex receive sensory info, and management the muscular action of the other aspect of the body. The 2 hemispheres play a crucial role in higher mental functions as well as language, process, and integration of sensory info, planning, higher cognitive process, and reasoning.

GENETIC INFLUENCES ON BEHAVIOR

Why folks react in an exceedingly bound way? We tend to don't have even a definite declare this question as a result of human behavior and characteristics are influenced by multiple factors. Currently, the 2 most vital factors that affect the behavior of the soul are their sequence and surroundings. Initial is that the familial issue and second is non-inherited

All the living being is completely different and distinctive. Each individual's makeup is the result of the interaction between genotype and surroundings. Though the sequences are also joined to bound traits it's unlikely that researchers can ever notice one gene that's entirely liable for most complex behaviors. Even the foremost extremely hereditary traits, like height, are influenced by environmental factors, as incontestable by ill-fed youngsters that are short despite having tall oldsters. During this example, environmental factors like nutrition intake have truly altered the means within which genetically influenced characteristics are expressed.

The present genetic theory has been shown in the U.S. that characteristics of oldsters are transmitted into the youngsters are through genes. They will be visible characteristics or maybe carried for potential transmission to a different generation as we will see that the youngsters of 1 set of oldsters don't inherit all identical characteristics.

This method of inheritance relies upon the very fact that offspring receives one in every of every sequence combine from every parent. A number of the genes are dominant and a few are recessive. Just in case of {recessive sequence|gene|cistron|factor}. Its characteristic does not show simply or unless each gene combines is recessive. On the opposite, a gene for a specific characteristic displays that characteristic, whether or not only 1 or each gene within the combine is dominant.

Further, the analysis of this a part of biological science goes on underneath the strict management of ethics. The analysis is essentially aimed to resolve the matter of genetically transmitted diseases or behavioral abnormalities. Moreover, through genetic manipulation scientists are attempting to regulate bound unwanted behaviors and to facilitate the required behavior.

MIND, BRAIN, AND CONSCIOUSNESS

Mind originates within the duality of consciousness; it breaks the consciousness into 2 associate degreed acts as an organ of communication between 2 communication systems. There is a unit of different definitions of mind in scientific and philosophic literature. It's all the scheme properties. As consciousness is a freelance of area and time, therefore, is also mind.

In philosophy, the mind is that the original sensory receptor and vital functions of mind area unit:

• Deliberation on totally different selections (sense mind),

• Discrimination and deciding (intelligent mind),

• Anchoring sensation and call to conditioned might be that that induces consciousness (Purusha) to spot with nature (Prakriti). The existence (ego-mind),

• Storage, retrieval and recollection (Chitta mind).

The theory of mind (TOM) simply implies that the acting person understands that the opposite person with whom the communication is established additionally possesses a mind. In TOM, the terms mind and consciousness are used synonymously. Someone in communication with another will browse the mind of the opposite person in terms of content and deliberation. Even a newborn will browse the 'mind' of his/her mother by looking at her gaze. This might be the start of understanding the other's mind as so much because the 'local' communication (communication in area and time) thinks about it. Language, verbal or nonverbal, is very important within the development of this ability to acknowledge and skim the other's mind.

THE EXTRAORDINARY PROPERTIES OF BRAIN

There is a unit some extraordinary properties of the brain, few of them {we can|we will|we area unit able to} take into account shortly here are the following:

- The brain is that the sole organ of the body that grows in each horizontal and vertical direction could also be it's meant for the corporatization of each dimension of nature, the horizontal and vertical.

- The brain is vertically open. Its animal tissue neurons area unit hospitable data within the supracervical domain.

- It is the sole organ of the body that is connected to dreams, imagination, and perception. Most likely it's still hospitable nature through transcortical routes!

- Unlike alternative very important organs like heart, urinary organ and liver, a minimum of some a part of the brain go to the remaining section (sleep) sporadically. If one is compelled to stay awake on the far side a vital amount of your time, one loses saneness.

- The brain seems as a seat of awareness; actually, it's the foremost unconscious organ of the body. Except in its 3 covering there's not any reasonable receptor for any reasonable sensation within the brain. It somehow corrects the old saying that conquest of the brain is that the conquest of the 'unconscious' could be right.

CONSCIOUSNESS

Our aware expertise is the consequence of a process of knowledge that we tend to receive from {different|totally different|completely different} sense modalities or no matter what we tend to expertise is the product of contributions created by different sense organs that produces the feeling.

We become awake to the planet around the North American nation through our consciousness. Consciousness could be a state of awareness of external and internal events knowledgeable by a personal. In normal waking state (consciousness) we tend to area unit awake to what's occurring around the North American nation, we tend to area unit awake to our thoughts, feelings, desires, perceptions, etc. On the opposite hand, if one falls unconscious because of low pressure, one isn't awake to all that's happening around the person. Once this person gains consciousness, he/she doesn't recognize all that was being done to revive him/her.

Consciousness is that the ground reality of an individual's nature. As per the scientists, it's neuro-centric that is focused on neurons inside the brain even it might be brain certain or brain freelance. Consciousness is we will refer to as the science of awareness, awareness of your thought, sensations, feeling, memory and atmosphere. One amongst the construct behind consciousness is body-mind philosophy that's supported the factor that body and mind area unit separate entity so that they act.

Psychology studies the conscious performances while many of them which are falling to physiology are not of such kind. For example, we can say that digestion is unconscious; the heartbeat is also unconscious unless it is not disturbed, and therefore, we can say that psychology is the study of conscious activities. We can even contradict it by some case, which is in the first instance conscious but later it is unconscious. In describing the relation between brain and consciousness the person prefers the speculation that consciousness emerges from a gaggle activity of countless neurons.

CHAPTER 7: SOCIAL MANIPULATION STRATEGIES

Here are some of the most powerful strategies for manipulating people in social or public settings and scenarios.

1. CASH IN ON THE HOME COURT

Ever noticed why several network marketing professionals always insist that you come to their home or office for a presentation rather than giving you a presentation in your home? There is a simple manipulation strategy behind it. When you negotiate within a physical space that belongs to you, subconsciously you are in a more authoritative position.

This is one of the biggest social manipulation secrets that few will tell you about. You have greater influence, control, power, and dominance when you are in a physical space that is your domain. It reflects in your body language, attitude, words, and actions. The place can be anywhere from your home to office to car, which you are comfortable and familiar with. Network marketers are always attempting to cash in on the home-court advantage, which is why they will insist that you come over for a presentation to their place.

When you are signing an important deal or negotiating terms of a critical association, always persuade the other party into coming over to your office or home for a talk. The comfort and familiarity of your space will put you in a position of greater confidence and authority, thus increasing your chances of cracking the deal in your favor.

Tell people that they need to understand the process or you need to explain everything to them in detail, which is why they should come over to your place. This is the angle you present to them. The reality is that you are giving yourself a higher position by conducting negotiations in a space that you own and are therefore familiar and comfortable in.

2. DISTRACTION STRATEGY

This is one of the most common manipulation techniques used by governments, political parties, world leaders, politicians, and other public personalities to divert the public attention from the vital problems by introducing continuous distractions and trivial/unimportant information.

This way, the public attention remains fixated on insignificant issues while the true political and social issues are hidden under the carpet. It gives the public the illusion of being busy with something, though that something is of little consequence in their life. They don't have the time to think about the negative impact of important issues in their life and the inability of their leaders to resolve these issues.

3. CREATE PROBLEMS THAT DON'T EXIST AND OFFER SOLUTIONS

This is another classic social manipulation strategy that is widely used throughout the world. It consists of creating an imaginary or foreseen issue to stimulate a specific reaction among victims of manipulation or the public. Then, the manipulator carefully introduces a solution to become the ultimate messiah.

For example, allowing urban violence to build and thrive initially or supporting terrorist camps. This can be followed by making people aware of how their security is the government's prime concern and how leaders will go all out to intensify security measures to ensure public safety.

You introduce a problem and then offer a solution for the problem without letting the victims realize that you were directly responsible for creating the problems. This way, you become the solution provider, who can get people to act in a desired manner.

4. THE PAINFUL REALITY

Let us consider a scenario to understand this strategy clearly. Your boss urges everyone at the workplace to put in additional hours of work or work during weekends. He/she may lead you to believe that you all stand to lose your jobs and the market is tight, which means that you have to step up and go the extra mile to survive. They will inform you about how other companies who weren't able to bag big projects couldn't sustain operation costs and eventually closed down.

The managers will convince you about how a few sacrifices from your side can go a long way in saving the company's fortunes. Do you see what they are doing there? They are projecting their decision as painful yet necessary. They'll tell how they don't want you to stay late at work, but there's no other option if you want to keep your job or the company has to stay afloat.

A majority will resign to the idea of working late.

5. TO PROJECT VICTIMS AS IGNORANT OR STUPID

The easiest way to get people to do what you want them to do publicly, professionally, or socially is to make them feel how ignorant or stupid they or how they don't understand something. For instance, if you are looking to introduce new technology that will save labor costs and increase profits, it may have a bunch of people rebelling against it for fear of losing their jobs.

By using the ignorant manipulation tactic, you inform people about how they cannot comprehend technology, which is designed to make things easier. You are playing on their lack of awareness or uncertainty about a thing. You are telling them that they aren't in a position to give their view or opinion about it because they do not have the right knowledge or understanding of these systems.

Again, you are replacing revolt with guilt by making the victims feel like they are responsible for their unfortunate situation or their lack of intelligence/capabilities. Thus, instead of rebelling, workers blame or devaluate themselves, thus inhibiting further action.

6. FOOT IN THE DOOR STRATEGY

This technique dates back to the times of door-to-door salespersons (hence, the name). To prevent people from shutting their doors on their faces, the salespersons use to put their foot in the door and request a couple of minutes to speak to the homeowners.

Once they got those 2-3 minutes with the homeowners, they would build upon it and try to sell their products to them.

Thus, in a social or public setting, this is one of the most effective manipulation techniques because it gives you that tiny opening, which you can cleverly encase on. You attempt to break the ice by making a small request from the other person that they generally won't refuse. This is followed by the actual or bigger request. What you are doing by asking for a smaller request to be fulfilled in putting you gently in the door and triggering a series of positive replies.

Once a person agrees to a small request, it is more challenging to follow it with a refusal. The trick here is to request for something tiny and reasonable that the victim can easily fulfill. This is to be followed by the actual intended or larger request.

7. DROWN THEM WITH FACTS, INFORMATION, AND STATISTICS

Emotional manipulation doesn't work on everyone, especially in social and professional settings. Here, people are more inclined to follow the logic and rational arguments. Drown these folks in information by quoting research, facts, figures, statistics, and more.

Have numbers ready on your fingertips for any objections and clarifications. Overwhelm people with statistics, logical arguments, and research. Be armed with the vital information to "intellectually bully" people. Present yourself as the ultimate authority or the source of knowledge in a particular field. Cleverly present research that supports your stand or point of view. Take advantage of established expertise to the fullest.

One of the best ways to manipulate people with logic is to present research, statistics, and figures in a compelling and imposing manner. Focus on areas where you believe they may not have sound knowledge and question them about it. This establishes their weakness in their own eyes. They will realize that they have little or no information about this area and that you are more experienced or knowledgeable than them.

This will automatically increase your chances of getting them to do what you want them to. This technique works well during business negotiations, sales, social debates, and other social or public settings.

You gain a smart subconscious edge over the other person, which makes them more defenseless and open to listening to you. It creates a sort of intellectual superiority, which makes them feel inadequate and compels them to comply with your demands.

8. THE VICTIM TALKS FIRST

When you are getting another party to agree to your negotiation terms or buy from you, allow them to talk first. This allows you as a persuader, influencer, or manipulator to establish their baseline. What are their strengths and weaknesses? What are their thoughts, emotions, fears, and behavior patterns? Are they more hesitant or self-confident? Do they appear extroverted/open or introverted/closed? Are they approaching the deal or sales with an element of hesitation? Are they overwhelmed by your presence? How does their body language reveal about them?

Allowing them to communicate first helps you set a baseline for both their strengths and weaknesses, which can be utilized to get them to act in the desired direction. You can also prepare a list of questions that you can ask them to establish a baseline. The idea is to get them thinking in the direction of taking action in your favor. For instance, if you are planning to sell insurance, you ask them a list of questions that help you establish their fears and therefore allow you to play on these fears for getting them to sign up quickly.

9. KILL TRUST ISSUES BY SHARING SOMETHING PERSONAL

A lot of people are wary of being manipulated because they've been misled or manipulated in the past. They come with a baggage of trust issues and always operate with a hint of suspicion. Such people are potentially difficult to manipulate since they always have their guard on.

However, one way to overcome trust issues or help them drop their guard is by sharing personal information. This makes them lower the walls and increase their trust in you. Ensure that the information you share is confidential or personal enough to break the trust barrier. Share something that they can relate to or they need to know to make the strategy even more effective. The information you share may be real or fabricated. However, the other person must believe it.

10. BE A MASTER AT DEBATES AND PUBLIC SPEAKING

It is about being able to persuade or influence people into taking the desired action. If you want to develop your persuasion or people-convincing skills, sign up for a public speaking class. You will learn to put across your point in a gripping, impactful and assertive manner without getting aggressive or pushy.

Notice how some of the best public speakers or orators can hypnotically charm people with their verbal and nonverbal communication skills. They use everything from their words to gestures to posture to voice tone to persuade people into thinking or acting like them. Convincing people takes a confident and powerful persona.

When you portray a confident and imposing personality, people automatically sit up and pay attention to what you are saying. Attract people like magnets by learning powerful strategies for appearing more convincing and presenting ideas in a more attention-grabbing/spellbinding manner.

To enhance your theatrics and/or communication skills, sign up for a theater or drama workshop. One of the greatest challenges in manipulating people is not just controlling your emotions and expressions but also having complete control over your body language, gestures, and expressions to portray the desired feelings or emotions. If you don't want to sign up for an acting class or theater workshop, study the mannerisms of actors. Examine the way actors express emotions.

Notice how they use the tone of their voice to create the desired impact. Observe how they pause at the right places to allow the significance of what they said to sink in. This should give you a good idea of skills you need to develop as a master manipulator or persuader.

So, you may be really happy that the person is about to do what you want them to. Yet, you may have to portray a different emotion to control the emotion of elation. Manipulating speech, expressions, gesture, posture, tone of voice, and other similar verbal and nonverbal communication patterns require practice.

Contriving emotions becomes easy when you can complement them with matching nonverbal clues. For example, have you practiced looking dejected and hurt when you don't get what you want? How about faking certain emotions when you clearly don't feel them?

Signing up for a drama, acting, or theater workshop makes you adept in honing your speech and acting histrionics, which are vital for boosting manipulation or persuasion powers. Haven't you observed how salespersons resort to extreme histrionics when they want to get you to buy something? Their body language, gestures, and expressions are amusingly exaggerated.

One of the biggest qualities of a master manipulator is that they have total control over their emotions. They don't allow their emotions to rule them. Actively practice controlling your emotions if you want to manipulate or influence people successfully. At times, people influencers or persuaders have to shed tears at the drop of a hat or laugh according to the situation. You will have to build a variety of emotions or expressions, which is a vital skill from the manipulation perspective.

11. TWEAK THE ENVIRONMENT TO GAIN ADVANTAGE

You can use the right environment at the right time to ask for someone to do something for you. Debunk the theory that there is a place and time for everything and make the environment work in your favor.

For instance, if you are partying with a boss or coworker on a Friday night, instead of waiting until Monday morning to ask them for a favor, use the relaxed setting of a pub or bar. They'll be less guarded, more chilled out and relaxed, and in a more positive mood. Your chances of getting them to agree to the favor may be higher in a more relaxed setting where they don't expect you to ask for such a favor. Change the setting of where you'd normally ask something like this to increase your chances of getting people to agree.

CHAPTER 8: RECOGNIZE EMOTIONAL MANIPULATION IN RELATIONSHIPS

he first year of their relationship was perfect. Barrett was everything Susan had ever dreamed of. They went on vacations and Barrett even went to Thanksgiving at Susan's parents. After that first year came to an end, things start to change. Barrett started to demand things from Susan. He stopped giving you any attention, he asked for money and used her house to throw parties. If Susan refused to give him something, Barrett fought and would ignore her for days. All Susan wanted was the good days during their first year, so she tried everything to make sure Barrett was happy.

After two more years of the relationship, Susan eventually realized that Barrett was controlling her life.

Manipulation in relationships is a big issue for many, and it doesn't happen in just romantic relationships. Family members or friends can control and twist a person's emotions. You are stuck living in the false hope of reaching perfect relationships with them. This is why it takes so long for a person to realize they are being manipulated.

MANIPULATION IN ROMANTIC RELATIONSHIPS

Out definition of manipulation referred to deliberate acts to control people. However, when it comes to romantic relationships, people will sometimes manipulate each other unintentionally as well. Whether conscious or not, it is still toxic and for a person's life and mind.

1. How are you living your life?

Do you live yours or theirs? A romantic relationship is about sharing each other's life. Manipulative partners bring you into theirs and make you disconnect from your own. Think about this:

- If you are friends with your partner's, is your partner friends with yours?

- How often do you go out to your favorite places?

- Did you move into their house or apartment?

When they bring you into their surroundings, they can control you more easily. Since you aren't comfortable within those surroundings, you do things according to the will of your partner.

CHAPTER 9: PSYCHOLOGICAL MANIPULATION IN THE WORKPLACE

When you think about your dream office environment it likely has a lot of people walking around happy and working well with each other. Good guys spread kindness with big smiles and comforting clothes. The bad guys can easily be spotted by their scary clothing and their evil attitude.

In the real world, nothing like this happens. You might feel like a superhero when you walk out of a movie theater, but your co-workers aren't going to be as open and honest. You can't easily decipher the good guys from the bad guys.

Everybody may greet you with a smile. Some of those smiles come from friends. You talk with them a little, they listen to what you say, and you feel that they understand you. They laugh at your jokes and you share some secrets and insecurities with them. However, you may end up discovering that one or two of those "friends" were trying to ruin you.

These people pose a lot of danger to your professional life because they aren't reaching a single ultimate goal. Ruining you is what they love. Messing with your office dynamic is what provides them with pleasure. At every step along your path to success, you will discover these manipulative people who turn your success into their success. They take risks and use everything in their power to control your actions and emotions. If you're surrounded by these types of co-workers, they can end up leaving your feeling worthless.

If these types of manipulators are prevalent in real-world offices, how are we supposed to protect ourselves from them? Is it inevitable that we end up being trapped by these sociopaths and low our self-esteem and dignity?

Let's take a look at what you can do to spot workplace manipulation so that you can respond to it correctly.

TYPES OF WORKPLACE MANIPULATION

- **Boost in confidence and hope**

"There has never been such a smart professional like you. I am going to make you the best employee."

This is the first form of manipulation that you will face when you join an office. The manipulative team leaders or bosses will try to include in their groups. They will try to get you to look up to them so that they can exploit your abilities. You could do something as simple as a search online for something and they shower you with compliments.

After the compliments, you start to receive messages from important people. They use your talent to help them build their careers. They make you think that you can become better if you work under them and do everything that they tell you to do in fact, most of these people either don't have the talent or they procrastinate, so all they are interested in is having you complete their work.

- **Flaw projection**

"Never have these mistakes been made in the history of this office. How could you be so careless?"

Manipulators will hide their inefficiencies and un-productivity by projecting their flaws. They will change the blame towards you so that their inefficiency stays hidden.

"This project can't be saved because I thought you could do it and turn control over to you."

"I made these mistakes because this project wasn't meant for me. You didn't manage this right."

The blames game is extremely common in workplaces where there are people who don't want to do their job and they try to hide their worthlessness. The plan is to twist reality so that their faults are hidden by bringing their victim into a negative spotlight. You are left trying to figure out how it is your fault while the manipulator shifts the blame from them to you.

- **Wrecking confidence**

"You're doing great, but it could be better."

Manipulators want to hit you and shake you up, but if you start to reach your expectations, it could cause you to feel confident so they will pull you down now and then to destroy your confidence.

No matter how great you do your job, or how logical your reasoning is, your work is never going to be appreciated. Even if they do appreciate what you do, it will be accompanied by a flaw.

"You handle your home and work life so well. That's impressive. But, you know, it is easy for single people to manage their home and work life, right? You do live alone? Oh, your parents live with you. Aren't you too old to be living with your parents? Being married builds character and teach to a person the responsibility. But, you shouldn't get married. It will cause you to lose your work focus."

This is the kind of thing you can expect to hear from a manipulator. They can define your entire personality by your marital status. Your success, work, and qualification don't matter.

- **Cruel sarcasm and hurtful jokes**

"It took you over five hours to finish this evaluation. A blind person could have done it half the time."

Cruel sarcasm and hurtful jokes can be aimed at you when you least expect it. They will likely come at a time when you would expect praise or some notice of your effort. Manipulators, however, will use these chances to make themselves look better than you and to make you end up feeling like a fool.

Manipulators will typically say something sarcastic in front of others. The other people will laugh which validates the statement and will ruin your moment. This is done deliberately to destroy your ability to work there. Some people are just sarcastic, but they don't use sarcasm as a means to destroy a person.

"Do you put together the presentation I asked for? You did. What are you waiting for then, Christmas? Send that to my email. Do you have experience sending an email? CC the boss, his wife, his servant, and the dog. In fact, just CC everybody in the office."

When you are faced with these types of comments, working becomes a lot more difficult. You are faced with negative energy the moment you step into the office and this isn't conducive for productivity.

- **Play victim**

"The whole office just wants to see me fail. You are my only ally."

It's normally your co-workers or team members who act like this. You feel bad for them because you see that others do treat them badly. Somehow, you seem to be around whenever they are complaining about not getting paid for their hard work. You know all about their problems and you have a good understanding of why they are having a hard time completing their work. This causes you to pity them so much that you offer to help them.

"My grandma had to go to the hospital. My parents are with her, but she wants to see me. Can you finish this up for me, but don't send it over to the boss. Send it to me."

Guess what? They have just tricked you and you are stuck working until late into the night. Plus, you aren't getting paid for this extra work. You're lucky if you get a thank you.

These are just a few of the types of office manipulators. Let's see how you can deal with the different manipulators in your office.

How to Deal With Office Manipulators

- **Criticizer**

The criticizer always minimizes what you do. They judge you and label you. They are direct with their criticism because "Criticism improves performance." This leaves you feeling ashamed and under-confident.

How to deal with this type of manipulator: This type of person will always find some way to criticize you. You need to try to understand those in your office who always criticize you. Stop taking them seriously. Tell them, "I will accept what you have to say if you politely approach me." Don't allow them to continue to disrespect you. Allow only the relevant criticism. If they bring in your personal life, remind them that they don't control your life.

- **Bully**

These manipulators have an aggressive response to everything you ask them, especially if you are questioning their work. They will resort to yelling and shouting before considering the whole scenario. They want to make sure that you leave them alone.

How to deal with this type of manipulator: Stand firm when they respond aggressively. Keep calm and present them with the facts to prove your point. They will keep up the aggressive act for a bit, but if you stay direct, they won't be able to take control over you. A bully's reputation is important to them, so if you respond with, "This is how we behave in a professional environment," this will give you power over the manipulator's manipulation.

- **Attention Diverter**

These manipulators are great at shifting the conversation to suit their needs. If a topic comes up that threatens to expose their faults, they will effortlessly change the subject. They are great at making irrelevant things relevant.

How to deal with this type of manipulator: You own your own emotions and insecurities and it's up to you how much you let others see that. When you notice a person trying to divert your attention, speak up. Insist that the conversation remains relevant and on the topic that it needs to be on.

- **Distorter**

These are the most common and most dangerous manipulators you may notice in your workplace. They don't use emotions. Instead, they distort facts. They gain as much information as possible from people around them. Then they start sharing information in a controlled and slow manner so that they get what they want.

How to deal with this type of manipulator: This person distorts information, so in order to save yourself, you need to make sure you have just as much information. Stop trusting what other people tell you and do your research to find out the truth.

- **Drama Creator**

These manipulators have an over-the-top answer for every situation. They like to manipulate and play with a person's emotions. If you have a manager that acts this way and you question them about their performance, they may respond with, "I have spent years with this company and given it my blood, sweat, and tears. What gives you the right to question my judgment?" They will also show up even when you aren't trying to interrupt what they are doing.

How to deal with this type of manipulator: You need to have factual intelligence to deal with this person. Always present facts when you are speaking with these people.

CHAPTER 10: DARK MANIPULATIVE PERSUASION

What is dark manipulative persuasion and how does it work?

Over the years, we have concluded that persuasion is positive while manipulation is the exact opposite. That is not entirely true. Whether you are persuading or manipulating a person, the real difference is your intention. According to some of the scholars studying the difference between manipulation and persuasion, three components are determining what a person is doing.

1. What intent lies behind your desire to persuade another person?

2. How truthful and transparent is the process you are using?

3. What is the net impact or benefit of your actions on the other person?

There is manipulative persuasion and dark manipulative persuasion. The first type, manipulative persuasion normally involves attempts to convince another person to do something without necessarily thinking about tactics or specific motivations. Anyone can easily use manipulative persuasion because it is not entirely necessary for the manipulator to understand his/her victim. A persuader will mostly look for ways to make the best out of the people he/she is manipulating. For instance, a politician can try to prevent war by creating peace ties where there were none. He/she might not fully understand the results of the ties, but will try anyway. A manipulative persuader can try to grasp at straws wildly hoping to get something.

On the other hand, dark manipulative persuasion involves understanding the bigger picture and strategizing. The dark persuader understands the person he/she is trying to persuade, knows the exact buttons to push and just how far he will go before getting results. In most cases, manipulators who use dark manipulation techniques are unconcerned with the morality of their actions. All he/she wants is to fulfill his/her desires regardless of the situation.

The bright side of dark manipulation is that the manipulator is in most cases aware of what he/she is doing. All of us have manipulated others, knowingly or unknowingly. There are many things we do to get what we want and in most cases, they are harmless.

It is said that we as human beings have learned how to manipulate each other selfishly. Sometimes it is necessary but in most cases, you will realize it is unnecessary. Dark manipulative persuasion often harms. Perhaps the most unfortunate thing is how the manipulators using dark techniques ignore the damage of their actions. For instance, many researchers conducted across the world over the years have revealed the harmful effects of smoking cigarettes. However, the manufacturing companies still make some successful manipulative advertisements leading people to think that this drug is 'cool'. Consequently, the number of diseases and deaths resulting from this manipulation increase. Those politicians using dark manipulative persuasion techniques to raise into position can facilitate weakened democracy and even foment division. Other campaigns use dark manipulative social tactics to support unhealthy and abusive relationships.

The reason why most of us cannot escape the trap of dark manipulation is that we fail to understand the situation logically and rationally, instead, we use emotions. For instance, supposing Rosy left a 2-year relationship because the partner was abusive even though he was faithful. A good number of people would be crazed because Rosy left a 'faithful partner'.

Another group would be happy because Rosy left an abusive partner, therefore, she is better off now. At one moment, rosy wants to reconcile with the partner. Then her friends discourage her by mentioning how ruthless, abusive and even secretly unfaithful the man was. The friends make up a story of how they had seen that man with other women in hidden places but had avoided telling Rosy. This makes Rosy not to make up with the boyfriend.

Rationally thinking, Rosy would rather be alone than with an abusive spouse. If she was your sister or mother, chances are, you would tell her to quit the relationship. However, some people will focus on the part where the friends made up stories and even prevented rosy from going back to the 'faithful' man. Did the friend do well by manipulating Rosy? Can you still classify this kind of manipulation as morally dubious or would you do the same if I was your friend involved?

It is true to say that Rosy's friends could have used other morally right and non-manipulative techniques to help their friends but what if they did not work? Can we then say that the end justifies the means?

THE DIFFERENCE BETWEEN MIND CONTROL AND MIND MANIPULATION

Some definitions of mind control equate it to mind manipulation. In one article on decision-making confidence, mind control is also manipulation, brainwashing, thought reforming, coercive persuasion, mental control, coercive control, malignant use of group dynamics among others. From this definition, we can agree that mind control is about influence and persuasion.

There is an element of control in manipulation and the vice versa is also true. In both manipulation and control, changing behaviors and believes is involved. Some people will argue that everything in life is manipulation. But if mind control is the same as manipulation, does it mean that we do not make any decisions freely? In stating that everything is a result of manipulation, a very important distinction is lost. So, what is the difference between mind control and mind manipulation?

First, human beings are very capable of dreaming big, even on an individual level. Furthermore, they have the capability and potential of making their dreams come to life by working collaboratively. People have achieved a lot over the years by working together. From finding God's particle to building pyramids and airplanes, the human mind has achieved unimaginable goals. So far, no animal is capable of achieving as much as we have the humans have high scales of coordination and efficiency.

The very nature of any coordination is a product of hierarchical set up of life and organizations. That is, for a company to be successful and effective, there has to be ranks and titles. Who makes which decisions, and who implements them? Hierarchical order has become the nature and fabric of life. In all organizations, families, politics, business et cetera, some form of command center has to take the authority and oversee the development. In this chain of command, orders are passed from top to bottom. On the Brightside, hierarchy reduces chaos in society. Imagine how the world would be like if all the developments were happening without people to oversee the order of things? On the dark side, this hierarchy takes away freedom because of People at the top decides and others do. Any disobedience is punishable.

People at the top of this hierarchy normally operate with two main modes, manipulation or control. The two modes are used for one purpose- to drive subjects. However, the execution is entirely different.

IN NATURE

Control involves the power to direct other people. That is, a figure controls the mind of his/her subjects by force. Mind control is used when the victim has minimal ways of escape. For instance, if a person does not have a way of meeting basic needs such as getting daily meals, you can control their mind into doing whatever you want by simply promising to meet this need. That is why the intensity of control is inversely proportional to the difficulty of the escape from the boundary of influence. If this person has another way of getting his/her needs met, then you do not stand a big chance of controlling him/her. Mind control was used to keep slaves. They were made to believe that the only way they would survive was through working for their masters. Control an also involve force, fear, and threats, and there is no subtlety to it. After World War II Russians had a stronger control on East German and it grew stronger because every possibility of escape reduced. Even in relationships, a controlling partner becomes stronger as if the subject shows that he/she cannot walk away. Mind control does not require trust between the manipulator and the victim. Most of the control tactics are about power and boundaries.

On the other hand, manipulation involves more subtle techniques. A manipulator will influence the victim or the situation unscrupulously and cleverly. Mind manipulation involves knowing personal things about the victim. No one likes a nosy person therefore; a manipulator has to acquire the trust of the person he/she wishes to manipulate before striking. Also, manipulation normally has shorter life compared to mind control because the manipulator has to work fast before his/her plans are found out. However, the impact of manipulation is likely to last longer than that of mind control. The intensity of manipulation is directly proportional to the level of trust between the manipulator and the victim.

Below are some important distinctions you need to make about manipulation.

Firstly, manipulation is a subtle process meaning that the victim is not aware of the intentions of the manipulator and the extent of the manipulation taking place. As such, the victim will consistently think he/she is making the decisions himself/herself and will make a small and gradual change in his/her. This person will not realize that all decisions were made by the victimizer.

Secondly, mind manipulation is an insidious process meaning that it takes time and will seem harmless but the results can be devastating. There will be a lot of hidden deception, cunning, and trickery that might gradually cause harm. The person will be trapped.

Thirdly, manipulation does not happen overnight. Mind control can be done instantly so long as one has power over what the victim wants. Manipulation, on the other hand, needs strategies and calculations. You need to know the best method to use and the timeframe. The length of time will depend on the methods you are using, your skills in manipulation, the duration you are exposed to the victim, and other personal and social factors, For instance, It would take a shorter period to manipulate a parent you live with in the same house as compared to a lecturer you only meet for 6 hours a week.

Mind manipulation is sophisticated because the victimizer is considered a friend, teacher, parent or any other trusted person. Because of the nature of this relationship, the victim is not willing to defend him/herself. He/she will think that the person in question has good intention, therefore, offer all the information required. This private information is what the manipulator uses to make the kill. This subtlety also makes manipulation more dangerous than mind control. It can even be more effective than physical abuse, and torture. Although there is not physical torture involved in manipulation, the results can be intense. That is because control can change the behavior of a person for a while at least until he/she gets another better way out of the situation but mind manipulation will change the attitudes, believes, behaviors and thinking process of the victim. And the person being ~~mined~~ manipulated will gladly and actively participates in the change process, believing it is the best.

So, it becomes very hard for the victim to latter accept that the person they trusted was just using them. And that is why it is very hard to convince a person that they are being manipulated by that close person, for instance, a spouse. Even after the victim gets away from the manipulator, it becomes hard to let go of the new thinking patterns, behaviors and beliefs because he/she believes the decisions were personal.

On the other hand, mind control does not require 'hiding' of information. The controlling person can be forceful, direct and even point-blank open about his/her intentions. A wife who is being mind-controlled by the husband may or may not be aware of what is going on. However, she will be a victim as long as she believes there is no way out. Mind control will normally involve some form of force, property possession; a difference of perception, limited escape options, minimum retaliation, and every interaction will involve proofing that one has power over the other person.

Manipulation, on the other hand, will be all about trust, use of information and subtle techniques. It works on breaking the current identity of a person and creating a new one. Any mind manipulator exploits the trust of his/her subjects and the information gap. Master manipulators also ensure that hey first identify a vulnerable person. For instance, a person who is recovering from a really bad break up is a viable victim because moments of weakness reduce the resistance to believing distorted reality.

When it comes to freedom, mind manipulation and control have different effects.

Mind control tends to create an unfavorable environment for the victim by restricting freedom. It also ensures that the victims do not easily identify a way out of the situation. When a tyrant leader controls his subjects, he/she fears freedom because it will create hope in the victim giving them the courage to resist and break free. Freedom allows us to become creative and expand our horizon thus bringing out the genius in us. Mind control involves curtailing freedom.

Mind manipulation involves creating conditions that make the subject to take options they would not under other conditions. Although the victim is not aware of what is happening, he/she will follow the manipulator. N manipulation, the freedom of the subject is not restricted but the manipulator will ensure that his/her ideas sound good and viable. The manipulated person will not have the time to see through the lies.

SUSCEPTIBILITY

Due to the nature of mind manipulation and mind control, everyone is susceptible to one or the other depending on the situation. If a mind manipulator knows enough information about you to make you trust them, then he/she will use that. If a person who uses mind control techniques knows something they can hold against you, they will use it. It is wrong to think that you cannot be manipulated or controlled. Everyone can be a victim. If you believe that such things cannot befall you, then your chances of being a victim are higher. Why? Because you will be too carefree and not see the victimizer as he/she attacks you, more so if it is a master manipulator. That is why it is important to learn how to identify a manipulator and escape his/her grasp. This will be covered in a later topic.

EFFECTS OF DARK MANIPULATION

All of us use manipulation techniques at one point or the other to get what we want. It is also true to say that all of us have fallen victim to manipulation at one point or the other. Mild manipulation may not have any lasting effects but there are some tools and techniques that leave lasting and drastic effects. Manipulation will involve controlling the behaviors, emotions, feelings, and decisions of others. The manipulative person may achieve what he/she wanted but leave the victim in a very undesirable place in life.

Emotional abuse in an intimate relationship is known to leave the victim in mental and emotional pain. Some people feel hurt when they discover that the partner they trusted was using them so much so that they too become manipulative. The effects of dark manipulation are more insidious of the manipulator is zooming in on one victim for instance, a husband focusing on the wife. If a manipulation technique is harmful to the emotional, physical and mental health of a person, it should be stopped. There is no justification for manipulative behavior, and no one deserves to be with manipulative people. It has been found that most manipulators have a deep-seated fear of losing control, therefore, they will do anything to intimidate anyone who shows signs of vulnerability. However, this should not be an excuse for hurting others. We all have fears that could drive us to undesirable activities; no one should be excused for mistreating others, especially if it is a grown-up person. The victim manipulation can experience different negative effects depending on the technique used. They can range from physical, mental, and even emotional.

PHYSICAL EFFECTS

Though mind-manipulation does not include physical force, there is some psychological and emotional torture used. These forces will affect the victim, for instance, he/she may feel stressed, devastated, insecure, and might even go into depression. Then, these effects will affect the physical body. Some people are affected by a betrayal so much that they are unable to do normal daily activities. You will see the effects of what they have been through in

the way they change their behaviors for instance eating
and sleeping habits.

CHAPTER 11: HOW TO DEAL WITH A MANIPULATOR

You will encounter manipulative people in your life – there is no question about it. So, you must learn how to deal with them. There are two kinds of manipulators that you will deal with; those you can avoid (egg strangers, casual acquaintances, etc.) and those who are a permanent fixture in your life (family members, close friends, colleagues, etc.).

When it comes to strangers and casual accountancies, once you notice that they are manipulative, you can keep your interactions with them at a minimum. However, if it's someone close to you, dealing with them is going to be a lot more complicated, and it requires a lot of effort and commitment on your part.

HOW TO INTERACT WITH A MANIPULATIVE PERSON

When you encounter a manipulative person, the most important thing you can do is to keep your emotions in check and try to be as logical as possible. So, first, you need to stay calm. Manipulators know that they are more likely to get what they want when you react emotionally, so they'll do whatever they can to get a rise out of you or to emotionally destabilize you in one way or another.

So, the best thing you can do at that moment is to take a breath, calm yourself, and try to think clearly. For example, when a manipulator asks you to do something, he will keep pushing you because he wants you to say "Yes" right away.

He wants you to make an instant emotional decision because he knows that if you take your time, think things over, weigh the pros and cons before making a decision; you are more likely to choose an option that isn't in your own best interest. From this point on, you should be wary of any person who tries to force you to decide the heat of the moment.

Often, manipulators will try to create a sense of urgency (egg a salesman may try to tell you that he is running out of stock, or your partner might give you an ultimatum). Approach every interaction with the understanding that decision making (no matter how small it may seem) is an executive function and not an emotional one, so anyone who wants you to make an emotional decision is technically a manipulator.

To help people avoid making emotional decisions in the heat of the moment, some psychologists recommend the use of grounding techniques to deal with strong emotions. For example, if you feel stressed or anxious, you can ground yourself by focusing all of your attention on what you are feeling in your body at the moment (if for instance, your heart is racing, focus your mind on your racing heart; this will keep your mind from racing all over the place, and it will help calm you down).

Once you have your emotions in check, the next thing you need to do is learn to say a firm "No." Many of us find it difficult to turn people down outright. Even if we have every intention of saying "No," we tend to go out of our way to soften the blow for the other person, to the point that it sounds to them as though there is room for bargaining.

Manipulative people are well aware of this vulnerability, and they use it to push the envelope as far as it can go. If they detect any hint of hesitation on your part, they take it and run with it; they'll try to guilt-trip you, shame you, threaten you, and do anything else they can think of to turn your "No" into a "Yes."

You can try to use diplomatic language wherever it's necessary, but when you say "No" don't leave your statement open to interpretation. For example, if you say "I don't think I can do it" instead of "I can't do it," a manipulator will take it as a challenge to try and change your mind.

When interacting with manipulators, you also have to learn to assert yourself. Manipulators will use lots of techniques to keep you from voicing your opinion or asserting for yourself because they know that if you don't clarify your position, they will be able to co-opt your view and make decisions for you. During the conversation, when you try to make a stand on an issue, the manipulator will attempt to keep you from doing so by talking over you or interrupting you. When this happens, most people will let it go, and the manipulator will get it his way.

When manipulators want you to agree with them inadvertently, they may use "we "sentences to get you to feel like they are on your side, or even to speak for you in front of others. They may also speak in incomplete sentences, or ask you to confirm every assertion they make because they are trying to make you more agreeable. To counter ensure that you never let anyone speak for you. Where the manipulator is involved, always make sure that you use "I" statements (e.g., "I want" or "I disagree") to create a clear distinction between you and the manipulator.

HOW TO IDENTIFY MANIPULATORS

Manipulators seek to control others to get them to do what they want. They aim to exploit people by paying with their thoughts and feelings. With this in mind, it's possible to indemnity manipulators by their words, body language, and behavior.

If you meet a person who encourages you to reveal a lot of personal details while at the same time he is going out of his way to hide details about himself, chances are you are dealing with a manipulator.

You can also tell that you are dealing with a manipulator if the person's actions don't match his words. Manipulators want to win you over, so they'll tell you what they think you want to hear. They'll make lofty promises at first, but when it comes to following through with those promises, they'll leave you hanging. So, pay close attention to what people say and what they do, and try to see if there is a disconnection between those two things.

Manipulators will try to alter your reality and change your belief systems. So, you should watch out for people who tell you blatant lies, even if the facts are easily verifiable. For example, when you are starting to date someone, and you catch them on a lie, but they keep insisting that their version of events is the true one, you can be certain that this is just the beginning, and that over time, their lies will just get more blatant.

Manipulators undermine your grist on reality by telling constant lies. When you hear small but incremental lies over and over, you will get to a point where you start doubting your reality. In some cases, it can turn out so badly, that you start feeling as though you are losing your mind. This is a manipulation technique that's known as "alighting," and it's more prevalent than you might think.

When you notice that someone is telling obvious lies early in a relationship, your best course of action is to terminate that relationship and to get away from that person as fast as you can.

You can also tell if you are dealing with a manipulator if he or she plays the blame game or tries to make you feel guilty about pretty much everything. Emotional manipulators understand that they can leverage guilt to make people do things for them as a way of atoning for their mistakes. While manipulators may be good at hiding their true nature during the early stages of a relationship, "guilt-tripping" and the "blame game" are two of the things that they find rather difficult to conceal. To manipulators, these techniques are useful from the outset of a relationship, so they may use them without even realizing it themselves.

If something goes wrong on your date, manipulators will try to turn it into your fault, as a matter of record. Even if you are dealing with something that is entirely out of anyone's control, they will make logical leaps to conclude that you are the one to blame. Similarly, if something goes right, they will try to take credit for it. For every small thing that they do, they'll make sure that they point it out, and that you acknowledge that they are the ones who are responsible for it.

For manipulators, the point here is to keep score. From the very beginning of the relationships, they will make sure that there is a running tally of all the good things and the bad things, and they'll make sure that they are ahead on the list of good things, and that you are ahead on the list of bad things. This way, they can always have something to hold over your head in case they want to manipulate you.

So, when you start going out with someone, pay attention to their attitude towards score-keeping. A score-keeper is almost always a manipulator.

Manipulators have a way of overwhelming you emotionally, even if you have only known them for a short time. If you meet someone, and you get the sense that they are just "too much too soon," chances are you are dealing with a manipulator.

Love smothering is a common manipulation technique, one that you can detect early in a relationship. Here, the manipulator will shower you with gifts and signs of affection to make you emotionally overwhelmed. When you receive an overwhelming amount of affection, you are more inclined to lead with heart instead of stopping to think things through, so this increases the chances that you will fall for a manipulator.

Romantic gestures are great at the start of a relationship, but if you feel that they are excessive, you should consider the possibility that you are dealing with a manipulative person.

DEALING WITH MANIPULATORS WHO ARE A PERMANENT PART OF YOUR LIFE

If a manipulator had been in your life for a while, you might have already ceded some level of control over your life to him by now, so you have to start by regaining that control. First, you have to create and enforce boundaries in your life.

To set and enforce boundaries, you have to assess different areas of your life and set firm limits in all of those areas. You have to draw a line, and you have to make it clear to the manipulator that he or she is not allowed to cross that boundary. For example, you can set aside some "me time" and tell everyone that they are not allowed to bother you during that time.

Setting boundaries will help you reestablish your priorities over your life. If you have been a victim of manipulation, chances are the manipulator has spent months or even years establishing control over your life, so that by the point you know what's going on, he may have replaced your priorities with his own. You may find that you are using all your free time to do things he likes, and your interests have taken a back seat to his.

When you find yourself in such a situation, bouncing back can be hard, but it's going to require a lot of willpower and commitment on your part. Take stock of your own life. Create a list of all your values and reexamine all of them. Look at your belief system, and question everything that you believe about yourself; did you always hold those beliefs, or did you acquire them over time as you got closer to the manipulative person?

If you notice that your time is spent doing things that don't interest you, your belief system has been infiltrated by ideas that aren't originally yours, and that your long term values no longer seem to be the driving force behind your life, you need to create new boundaries and rules for yourself to keep the manipulative person from controlling you.

You need to disconnect from manipulative people, especially the ones whose machinations have caused you (or could potentially cause you) serious psychological or physical harm. One mistake most victims make is that they assume that they can change the manipulator. They convince themselves that if they spend enough time with the manipulator, he will fall in love with them, and he will be open to treating them better. However, in the end, the positive happens. Instead of the victim changing the manipulator as she may have hoped, it's the manipulator that changes her, and not for the better. She starts accepting the emotional abuse, and little by little, she makes concessions about her values and principles, until, in the end, she is a completely different person. She becomes more subservient, and she starts making excuses for the manipulator.

So, once you notice that someone is manipulating you, the best choice you have is to disconnect from them. If a clean break is possible, you should go for it. However, in situations where it's a lot more complicated (for example, where you have children together) a clean break might not be possible. Even then, spending some time away from the manipulator can help you re-enter yourself so that you can remember what your real values and priorities used to be.

CHAPTER 12: TIPS AND TRICKS TO DEFEND YOURSELF FROM MANIPULATION

Now that we have gone over some of the methods and tactics people use to negatively manipulate others, it's time to talk about how to avoid these methods. Negative manipulation can be defined as convincing others to do whatever you desire, without offering something of value back to them. How does this phenomenon work?

A Threat and no Value: If a person says, "Help me finish this project or I'm going to be angry with you," they are trying to negatively manipulate your actions. They are not offering anything of value to you in return. However, if a friend offers you something of value in return for a favor, that isn't negative manipulation, because you're getting something back for the effort you put in.

Making another Responsible for their Emotions: Another form of manipulation is telling someone that they are responsible for how you feel and that they should feel guilty for that. For example, telling them that if they don't come to your party, you will be highly disappointed. This implies that it's their fault how you feel. However, if you offer to introduce your friend to someone they have been wanting to meet at your party, you are offering a situation that allows both of you to win.

WHY DO PEOPLE MANIPULATE?

What are people's reasons for manipulating others?

Misery Likes Company: They do it because they gain satisfaction, on an emotional level, from seeing the frustrated or otherwise negative responses of others. Certain people are so unhappy with their lives and themselves that they try to bring others down by creating problems for them.

It makes them feel Powerful: Someone who is insecure and feels powerless will often try to exert power in other areas to make up for it. Getting others to do what they want gives them temporary satisfaction.

A Lack of Importance: Another reason why people negatively manipulate others is that they don't think that they are important. They believe that if they simply request what they wish for, they won't get it because they don't matter enough. So instead, they try to make us feel ashamed or guilty as a consequence for not doing what they want, as a preemptive measure from disappointment.

They are "too Good" for some Things: Other negative manipulators simply think that they are too good for certain tasks. They might see other people as below them, and therefore expect those people to do the tasks that they don't want to do. This could be due to laziness, or simply an inflated sense of self.

Not Knowing how to get Things done: Some negative manipulators don't think that they are capable of gaining what they want, and instead operate under the assumption that they must convince and pressure others to do their bidding for them.

Selfishly "Helping" Others: Other negative manipulators convince themselves that what they are doing will help people. This is a common idea embraced by people who think that they know better than others what is best for everyone. Due to their beliefs that they have a higher intelligence or ability, they feel satisfied doing this and convince themselves that the people being manipulated are better off for it.

The majority of negative manipulators are not bad people; they are simply misguided, inconsiderate, insensitive, selfish, and often, weak and insecure. Some of them believe that the people they are manipulating are not as valuable as themselves and that their desires and needs are not as important. This mistaken belief is what allows them to continue to act the way they do without considering the feelings of other people.

DIFFERENT TYPES OF NEGATIVE MANIPULATION

Turning your Emotions against you: Techniques for manipulation vary widely, but usually, negative manipulators will attempt to get the feelings of others to work against them. They will try to do that by doing or saying things that are intended to stir up fear, anger, shame, guilt, or any other uncomfortable feeling. For example, they might insinuate that if we don't follow through on their suggestions or orders, something horrible will result.

Threats of Future Unpleasantness: They might also try to describe to you all of the different types of unpleasant situations that could arise if you don't do what they want. They might imply or even overtly insist that something is our fault, responsibility, or duty, using ethics and morality to pressure us to come around to their ideas or demands. Some people will even throw every trick at us, warning us of the consequences of disappointing or letting them down.

Common Phrases Used: They may imply to us that we will be so happy if we do what they want us to do, or that we will make them very happy, and that they will love us so much. They may also use phrases like "You need to..." or "You must..." or "You should..." as a way to subtly pressure you into following through on what they are asking of you. They will say those phrases and others which insinuate great consequences if you don't follow the obligation they are giving to you.

What does each of the above methods and techniques share in common with each other? The person doing the negative manipulation doesn't offer anything of value in return for fulfilling their wishes. Instead, the victim gets exploited by a created power imbalance.

HOW TO AVOID BEING NEGATIVELY MANIPULATED BY OTHERS

Be Aware of Your Rights: The absolute most important rule you can follow when dealing with someone who wants to manipulate you in negative ways is to know your own worth and rights. This way, you will always know when someone is attempting to violate them. So long as others are not getting harmed in the process, you should be defending yourself. Every human should have the right to have differing opinions from others, to protect yourself, to say "no" when you need to, and to decide what's important to you. You should also have the right of expressing your wants, opinions, and feelings, and always be treated with respect.

Unfortunately, the world has plenty of people who won't want to acknowledge or respect your rights, especially negative manipulators. You will also come into contact with others who generally wish to take advantage of any opportunity. However, you can proudly defy this by letting them know that you are the one who runs your life, no one else.

Maintain Healthy Distance: Another way to tell who is manipulative is to pay attention to the way someone acts in varying situations and in front of various individuals. Although everyone, to a degree, puts on different faces depending on where they are, most people who are harmfully manipulative are extreme about it. They might, for example, be extremely polite and friendly to one person, and completely disrespect another, or act like a victim one second, and then act controlling immediately after.

If you notice someone acting this way regularly, it's a good sign to distance yourself from them and not engage with them unless it's an absolute necessity. Usually, the reasons behind these types of behavior are complicated, and it isn't your duty or responsibility to help or change that person. Trying to do so will often only lead to suffering on your part, so it's better not to expect much when you notice these signs.

Don't Blame yourself: A person who wishes to manipulate others in harmful ways searches for weaknesses to exploit, so it makes sense that someone who has been victimized by one might blame themselves or feel inadequate. But in a situation like this, you should remember that it isn't you that's the issue here; you are being pressured to feel bad by someone else who is very good at making people feel bad.

This is how they get their way. Instead, think about the relationship you have with this person and ask yourself if they are respecting you, demanding reasonable things of you, and whether you are both benefiting, or only one of you is. Ask yourself, also, if you feel good about yourself after spending time with this person, or if you would feel better being around them less. The way you answer these questions will lead to important answers about where the issue lies in the situation.

Questioning them: Eventually, this type of person is going to demand or request things from you. Many times, these requests or others will consider their needs, while completely ignoring yours. Next time you receive a solicitation that is completely unreasonable, turn the focus back to them by asking some questions. Ask them if their request is reasonable, or if what they are asking from you is fair. You can also try asking if you get to have an opinion in this matter, or ask what benefit you will be gaining from the arrangement.

Each time you ask questions like this, you are holding a mirror up to them, allowing them to see what they are truly asking of you. If they are self-aware, they will likely retract their request or demand. But there may be some cases, such as dealing with a narcissist, who will keep insisting without even considering your questions. If that happens, follow these guidelines.

Don't Answer Immediately: One way to combat manipulation is to use time as a resource. Often, the manipulator will not only ask you to fulfill an unreasonable demand, but they will want an answer immediately. When this happens, rather than answering right away, use time and distance yourself from their request and influence. This can be done by telling them that you will think about it. Although these words are simple, they give your power back to you, giving you the option to weigh the advantages and disadvantages of the situation and let you work out something better, if need be.

Teach yourself to say "No" when needed: Saying "no" is difficult for many people, since we are often taught and conditioned to be polite whenever possible. Being able to confidently but politely say "no" comes with learning communication skills. When this is articulated effectively, you can hold onto your self-respect, and also continue a healthy relationship. Keep in mind that your personal rights include deciding what matters to you, being able to turn down a request free from guilt, and choosing health and happiness for yourself. You are responsible for your life, not the person who is making unreasonable demands of you.

Create a Consequence: Next time a negative manipulator tries to violate your rights, and refuses to accept your answer, set a consequence for their behavior. Knowing how to assert and identify appropriate consequences is a crucial skill for standing down someone who is being very difficult or disrespectful. If you can articulate this clearly and thoroughly, your consequences will cause them to pause and stop violating you, shifting to a position of respect.

How to Confront a Bully safely:

Not all manipulators resort to bullying, but many of them do. Someone is being a bully when they use intimidation or harm to get what they want from you. Remember, always, that a bully chooses people they see as weak to pick on, and compliance and passivity will only strengthen this. However, a lot of bullies are afraid and insecure deep down, so when their victim starts to stand up for themselves, this will often lead the bully to back off. Whether this situation is occurring in a playground or at the office, it applies, most of the time. Keep in mind that many bullies have withstood bullying and violence. Although this doesn't excuse their behaviors, it does help the victim to understand.

Your Influence Skill Set

Clarity of purpose

An important facet of the ability to influence others is your clarity. Know what you want and have a clear plan of how you're going to get it. Whether you're working in sales and trying to improve the team's quarterly figures, or trying to encourage a student to be more diligent with study, or to set them on a career path – know what the objective is. The only way you can succeed in influencing someone to behave in a desired way is if you are clear about what you hope to achieve. You don't get in your car to drive to a destination you've never been without setting the GPS. The same goes for the application of influence toward achieving a desired effect or goal. Know where you're going.

Always be prepared in advance, with the following:

- A list of prioritized objectives.

- A clear picture of the final destination (what it looks like).

Preparing the environment

If you are seeking to reach an agreement with someone, you need to make them feel comfortable. You also need to be relaxed, yourself. At the same time, for effective communication (which is important when you want to influence someone's behavior, as this book is explaining) you need to make the environment conducive to your interaction. And you need to have in place a planned sequence of events at that meeting beforehand.

The best way to achieve this is to draw up a meeting agenda and circulate it to those who will attend, one day before the meeting. In this way, everyone knows what to expect and what shape the meeting will take. The agenda should make clear what the goals of the meeting are. Checking off the items on it should move you closer to the agreement, if not enable all present to reach consensus to move forward. The logical sequence of events represented by following an agenda is a function of a critically structured plan. Having a plan of such quality never fails to impress.

Consensus building

In building consensus, you're making it clear you are open to suggestions (which you should always be, regardless of your single-minded focus on your ultimate goal). Hearing what people say and truly listening means you're not planning a response while they're talking. It means you're actively hearing everything they say. Subtext, word choice, and tone are all important and so are your skills at hearing what's being said. Proceeding with these skills in play can provide you with the basis for genuine and not false consensus.

False consensus is reached when people are "heard out", but not "heard". These are two entirely different animals. The first is the condescending indulgence of hearing what no longer matters because a decision has already been made and the results of that decision, imposed. Being heard means that influence on the final decision is still a possibility and that what's offered may result in concessions, if it features actual merit.

Being present to the input of others and being able to integrate their thoughts and suggestions into an existing plan is a function of leadership. Leadership is not imposed. Leadership is extended to others as a service. Consensus building is a way to bring forward the knowledge of the team and add it to your own. In the case of reaching an agreement, it's the foundation of lasting relationships that won't later be ruptured by objections to not being heard. This is extremely important. Autocratic leadership is unwelcome and will not survive for long. It is a corrosive leadership style that is not sustainable.

Creating rapport

When someone begins to enjoy your company, it becomes much easier for you to enlist their support. This makes it more likely they'll support your viewpoint in situations in which that counts. Allies are people who like and trust you. Your relationships are what will move your goals forward and create a foundation for your success and that of your allies, also. People, while perhaps not being entirely aware of this on an intellectual level, know this instinctively. That is why you must prioritize establishing rapport with others. It's the basis of strong allegiances.

Part of creating rapport is establishing the common interests you hold with others. Taking an interest in them and offering them information about who you are is how this is achieved. Being too veiled about yourself makes you appear cold, calculating and detached. Establish that you're open and also, a person who can be trusted.

It's also important to establish easily with others and one way this can be done is to mirror the body language. You'll probably find (if you pay attention), that you do this anyway when you've begun to establish rapport with someone. Mirroring body language sends the unconscious signal that there is a bond already established between two people and that they're on the same team. Mirroring speech patterns is another way of doing this. Repeating keywords with enthusiasm at opportune times is another natural way we tell each other we're enjoying a conversation or agreeing with each other. Nod, smile and respond positively when you sense a common theme emerging in conversation. This sends the message that you're accessible on the most basic, human level.

Suggestions instead of demands

People routinely bridle at directives. In Western societies where individualism is a way of life, we like to believe in our autonomy as a value. That means it's not the best course of action to demand things from people. Much more effective is suggesting a course of action and building consensus based on the suggestion while being open to input and concessions to other points of view. This is the democratic way of achieving goals and one that is completely manageable with the application of a deft hand.

Here are examples of language that gives your listener the option to chip in and yet still leaves you the "wiggle room" to get to where you believe you need to go:

- Would you be interested in doing a-b-c?

- Could you be interested in doing a-b-c?

- I think we should do a-b-c. What do you think?

- Do you think this is the best way forward, or do you have other ideas?

Leaving space for opinion and input, while still advancing the validity of your own opinion is the stuff of which influence is made. While you're providing people with a rationale for your point of view, your willingness to entertain amendments to that point of view only increases your influential power. Imposition rarely ends in anything but resentment. By building consensus through input and exchange, you will still arrive at the goal you have in mind, but you'll do it with the support of a willing team, signed on to the plan in question. A fringe benefit? That input will undoubtedly improve on the original plan and will result in satisfaction on the part of all involved.

Heightening your awareness

Awareness of the responses of other people to what you're saying is a key to influential action. What are their facial expressions telling you? Their body language and word choices? What about tone and pitch? All these factors are rich with information that you can draw on to temper your pitch and get people on your side. It can also cue you to back off and change lanes, while you re-group and allow others their input.

Active listening, while employing body language (head nodding, eye contact) and assenting noises ("uh-huh", "yes", "I see") is also about deeply engaging with what's being said and the complementary messages being sent by the speaker. Your awareness in crucial situations, of all the factors that create a communicative environment, is of the utmost importance. You need to be aware, not only of what's being said but implications about what's intended, what's not being said and the speaker's frame of mind. All these factors work together to form a more concise body of information from which you may draw to apply influential action.

CONCLUSION

While outright mimicry is obviously out of the question, you can certainly seek to mirror the communication styles of the people you're engaging with, to help you establish rapport and common ground. Suppose someone looks at you for just a couple of seconds before looking down, or past you, and then looks back at you. This non-verbal style tells you something important about the person you're engaging – sustained eye contact is undesirable. So mirror that, to establish a comfortable level of communication that's implicitly agreed upon by both parties. This is an unspoken level of communication. By mirroring the tendencies of the other party, you are sending a message of respect and concession to the communication style being modeled.

After a business interaction, especially a meeting, you must provide a summation of what you came into that meeting intending to do. In the course of your summation, you can acknowledge the importance of the feedback and input the exchange or meeting has provided. Pointing out that the feedback received was pivotal to the development of your agenda and enriched it, gets people on your bus and ready to roll. When people feel their opinions are valued, they will come along for the ride. They will also form part of a team that is more cohesive than if you hadn't included and then acknowledged the role their input played in reinforcing your foundational agenda.

The addition of the input of others to your narrative is a key component of consensus building as a part of influential action. It's a form of leadership outreach that not only strengthens the leader's position but strengthens the agenda's integrity. Adding useful feedback and input can only build a better mousetrap. Good and successful leaders are keenly aware of this.

9 781708 609740